WHEN YOU LOSE SOMEONE YOU LOVE

By
RICHARD M. CROMIE, D. D., Ph.D.

Desert Ministries, Inc.
Palm Beach, Florida

WHEN YOU LOSE SOMEONE YOU LOVE

(Revised & Expanded 2001)
Third Printing
©Copyright 2001 by
Desert Ministries, Inc.
P.O. Box 788
Palm Beach, FL 33480
ISBN 0-914733-28-1

Printed by Eagle Graphic Services, Fort Lauderdale, Florida

Dedicated

to

Harry Marlin & Margaret Acker Cromie

and to

Fred Courtney Babcock

PREFACE

We at Desert Ministries, Incorporated are pleased to offer this book to you. It comes out of my four decades as an active parish minister, the most recent six years as Preaching Pastor of The Royal Poinciana Chapel, in Palm Beach, Florida.

It joins a long list of books and booklets from DMI, intended to provide help to pastors, laypersons and professional workers in the desert times of personal crisis and family change. Death is the worst of them all.

Several different authors have written for us. We choose the best-qualified people available, whose ideas and approaches are compatible with our philosophy and theology. We have booklets available on how to handle divorce, cancer, Alzheimer's, suicide, alcoholism, and many more. We also publish devotional booklets, one special one for those in hospitals and nursing homes, <u>Christ Will See You Through.</u>

All of these are available, as well as a complete list of our publications, on request to our office:

> Desert Ministries, Inc.
> P.O. Box 788
> Palm Beach, FL 33480

We will gladly send you a sample packet without charge. More information is available on our website: www\desmin.org. We survive and publish by the voluntary contributions of Board Members, friends, and those who use our materials.

Cordially,

Richard M. Cromie, D.D., Ph.D.
President, Desert Ministries, Incorporated

TABLE OF CONTENTS

INTRODUCTION

It happens soon or late: death intrudes on every life; the moment comes for everyone when you lose someone you love. As pastor I am often there, and several times I have been there by myself. Sometimes it comes suddenly and without warning. Sometimes it comes after a long and lingering illness. Sometimes it comes in a peaceful parting of one who has lived a good long full life. At times it comes by self-inflicted wounds. Sometimes its arrival is a mystery. But, it comes to everyone, young and old and to all the in-betweens. "Never morning wore to evening", Tennyson wrote, "but that some heart did break." It never does.

When it comes, especially at painful and unexpected times, the lives of the loved ones remaining are forever changed and often shattered. "Her death forced me to a new touch with finality", my learned professor friend murmured to me thirty years ago, "I can't believe she's gone." No one can. For a long time you keep expecting to see the one who has gone away.

This little booklet can be seen as a pastor's response to that final loss, and not only for my friend, but for all who have walked that lonely road, for those who walk it now, and of course for those who one day will. I have no magic potion to offer, no panacea, no secret password; but I have walked that way myself. It takes time and care to ease the pain and loneliness of separation. Readjustment does not come easily, the road is all uphill; it is rugged and steep, at times impassable.

Much of what I know about this subject has come when my own friends and family members died and left me pondering the next steps I needed to take. But, I have also learned by watching others in my forty plus years as minister. Seldom a week goes by but that someone in churches I have served, and in our Chapel now, passes away. Through the decades, those who remain have shared their worries, their regrets, their fears, their anger and their musings over all that might have been. My purpose here is to offer some broad range of ideas, and some specific suggestions too on the process we call grief. My hope is that it will be helpful to you and to others who need a hand to hold. I leave the rest to you.

My special thanks go to any and all who might identify something familiar in some item of their personal journey within these pages, although I have meticulously tried to avoid any specific reference to actual individual people or situations I have known. I respect pastoral confidences, totally. Those who have shared with me, talked and listened in the hours of grief have given me confidence to move ahead. I would never risk offense against their trust in me, even where the matter appears harmless.

I thank Fred C. Babcock for his help with the original of this book. He was one of my friends and fellow travelers for a long, long time. Fred is now gone. He was a charter member of the Board of Desert Ministries, Inc., back in 1983. His interest and support were always magnanimous, to say the least. The Babcock Charitable Trust provided the funding for the original publication. When Fred died, I asked his daughter Courtney Babcock Borntrager to take his place on our Board of Directors. Thankfully she accepted. When it came time to update and enlarge this book, Courtney volunteered to cover the cost of the new edition.

J. D. Thrower of Eagle Graphic Services in Fort Lauderdale has been most helpful to us in selecting the cover and planning the layout of both publications. We are most grateful for his interest in our work, for his dedication to the Lord, and for his expertise in this and our other publication endeavors.

Beverly B. Olson typed the original book. Martha Worth, a friend from Pittsburgh, and a part time staff member at The Royal Poinciana Chapel, now living in Florida, has been of enormous assistance in preparing this new and enlarged edition.

While many of our DMI publications have been widely used all around the nation, <u>When You Lose Someone You Love</u> has been by far the most frequently requested of all our past and current books. Dozens of pastors, lay callers and friends use it as an extended "sympathy card". Others use it as a "conversation piece" with a friend or family member who is reluctant to share personal feelings. It has gone through three separate editions prior to this enlargement.

One friend asked, "Why change it? People love it as it is." Well, I needed to add some useful ideas and items I have discovered since the last printing. A wise pastor never ceases to seek new and deeper understanding. God does not reveal all of his treasures at once. Also, some friends and readers have called to my attention areas I had overlooked, e.g. the death of a brother/sister, or a favorite poem I have mentioned elsewhere. The last chapter is entirely new and adds a broader dimension to the question of what happens when we die. My hope and prayer is that it will be helpful to you and to those you love. Meanwhile, God bless you and keep you in His care.

DR. RICHARD M. CROMIE, PH.D., D.D.
"The Sea Gull Cottage" at
The Royal Poinciana Chapel
Palm Beach, Florida
July 15, 2001

PART I

THE WORLD IS NEVER THE
SAME AGAIN . . .

The world is never the same again after someone you love has died. Never, ever. In one of Charles Dickens' short stories, there is the scene of an elderly woman standing with tears in her eyes at the grave of a man who had died at age twenty-five, fifty years before. The dates were still visible. A passerby came up to comfort her. Noticing the young age of the deceased and the five decades which had passed, the stranger said to her, "I am sorry, dear. Was this your son?" "No," she replied a bit impatiently, "He was my husband". . .! And a thousand years, the Bible reminds us, pass as a watch in the night.

Time is not what it is in other ventures when it comes to memories and grief. I have seen real live painful tears at five, ten, twenty, even thirty years after the death. Dickens apparently saw them at fifty. I have watched people grieve on endless anniversaries and birthdays, as if the parting had happened yesterday. "Our New Year's Eve has never been the same since 1942", she said, "when those two uniformed soldiers came to bring the awful news. They have all been special burdens since then."

From a personal point of view I can testify that twenty years is like a watch in the night. Back then our family had an awful year, to say the least . . .my brother Bobby died on April 15, 1985, at age forty-three. None of us could believe it. He had just made an offer on a house. His realtor called his home the next morning to tell him the good news. I was there, by then. Mother had called me to say that Bob had not arrived for work earlier that morning, and asked me to go over to make sure everything was O.K. I was providentially visiting Pittsburgh at the time. I went to his apartment. When the telephone call came from the realtor, I was already there and he thought I was Bobby. He said, "Congratulations, (I guess we sounded alike to Norm.) you are the proud owner of a new dwelling place!" I replied that I was not Bobby, but that he would never know how right he was. I had discovered a few minutes earlier that Bob had died sometime during the night. As they say in Scotland, he had "gone away" to the Lord, to a new dwelling place indeed! Income tax day never rolls around but that my first thought is not of Uncle Sam. It is of brother Bob.

By the way, it got worse. My father was so over burdened, trying to handle Bobby's death and other things, that on the following September the Fourth, he also died, without warning, in the wee hours of the morning. The next August the Fourteenth, my dear Mother decided that she had had enough loneliness for one lifetime. She passed away during the night a couple of days after they told her she had cancer. Oh dearie me: "The world is never the same again after someone you love has died . . ." Too much has gone away with the deceased.

> "With you a part of me hath passed away;
> For now in the peopled forest of my mind
> A tree made leafless by this wintry wind
> Shall never don again its green array.
> Chapel and fireside, country road and bay,
> Have something of their friendliness resigned;
> Another, if I would, I could not find,
> And I am grown much older in a day.
> But yet I treasure in my memory
> Your gift of charity, and great heart's ease,
> And the dear honor of your amity;
> For these once mine, my life is rich with these.
> And I scarce know which part may greater be,
> What I keep of you, or what you rob from me."
> SANTAYANA

The mighty force called grief comes in strange and impromptu ways, often in surprising and unexpected places. We read in the Song of Solomon, "Lord, save us from the little foxes which come under the fence." We can usually protect ourselves from the beasts of the field by keeping watch and building shelters here and there, and by erecting huge fortresses to keep out the thundering herds of danger. But as every farmer knows, especially the one who has a fence around his little garden, tossed up in haste perhaps . . .the little foxes sneak in during the night. They dig right under the fence. When the farmer least expects it, they steal away his produce. The little foxes will steal away your happy moments, too. Tears come at the oddest time without warning. Life is never the same again after someone you love has died.

This strange power called grief works its weary way in around the edges of your soul and psyche. "What's wrong with you?" I once heard a Grandmother bark to her little grandson just seven years of age. (She was the impatient kind.) What was wrong with him?. . . I could have told her: the little boy was grieving, in his own rambunctious way. To her a lot of time had passed since his mother died. But his grief was as real as the first day, sure as sure can be.

"What's wrong with my teenaged son?" the father asked me boldly. "He is making a mess of his life. Talk some sense into him, Reverend." I said the lad was grieving, for his mother who had died three years before, grieving for what was lost and never found again, grieving for the loneliness one feels when a parent has been taken, grieving for. . . I tried to help his father understand.

A season of grief can alter and stifle the course of a whole lifetime, especially if the time of grieving is not accomplished when it should be. It is so intense, and by the accident of not knowing what to do, or in the confusion and clatter of the unknown, or in the unresolved fears, all of those will follow you forever, unless you solve them now.

For example, I know a man, now in his early middle years, who was involved in a horrible auto accident when he was eighteen. Two young people, including his best friend, died in the crash. He was seriously injured, but he survived. I knew him then and I have known him ever since. He has never fully recovered emotionally from that dreadful day.

"Why is she so mean?" the daughter asked. "I've never seen or heard my mother talk that way before." I said, "She is grieving." Every time the funeral hearse goes rolling by, every time we touch base with another round of death, every time we have a bad dream . . .it all comes back, as if we were grieving for the first time, or the last. Grief waits at the end of every day. It's there when you enter the empty house or apartment. "I still expect her to be in there," Forrest told me, "every time I come home." It hangs around in the front row of your memories. It sits in the pupils of your eye to remind you: life has forever changed, and it will never be the same again.

I once had the privilege of being friend and pastor to a dear woman who lived to be one hundred and seven. I was invited to what turned out to be her last birthday party. After the songs and the candles, I asked her, "What is the most important thing for a one hundred and seven year old to remember?" She smiled and said, "I always try to live to be a credit to my father." He had died fifty-seven years before that day, but she never had forgotten what her father meant to her.

Grief crops up in strange and unpredictable ways. We are wise to know that and to try to remember it. If you act the fool, or if you find some meanness you did not know you had, or if your whole attitude changes toward life and death, whatever, pause and meet your grief. Make friends with it. Think about the good times. Lean on your faith. If your steady faith should falter, even fail you, try not to worry, it will all come back again when the proper time has passed. But, do not leave it unresolved. A young friend of Desert Ministries, Incorporated gave me this poem when her father died:

> Do not stand by my grave and weep.
> I am not there. I do not sleep.
> I am a thousand winds that blow.
> I am a diamond glint of snow.
> I am the sunlight on ripened grain.
> I am the gentle autumn rain.
> When you awake in the morning hush,
> I am the swift, uplifting rush
> Of quiet birds in circling flight.

I am the soft starshine at night.
Do not stand by my grave and cry.
I am not there...I did not die.

AUTHOR UNKNOWN

• • • •

"Johnny died and went to heaven," she once told me, "the rest of us have gone to hell".... "He's grieving for a father that he never had," the psychiatrist alerted me. Another said, "He is grieving for a child that was not born at all, grieving for a friend he lost a long, long time ago." When one young woman read this book, she said she was grieving for "the loved one" she never had.

• • • •

Once in a while that grief is associated with a child lost to abortion. I do not wish to raise the politics of that procedure here. I will leave that to others. I include it now for those who, trying to do what they felt was right at the time, and then later were left with a sad and troublesome memory. A middle aged woman I know said to me "Oh Reverend, I wish I had gone ahead and had my child . . . . He would be thirty-seven this holiday season. I often think about how he would have turned out." You can't go back again.

• • • •

The first time a person comes in contact with death, the memory can imbed itself forever in the soul and psyche. It is a monumental thing. I often ask those who have lost someone they love, and who are not inclined to talk or share their feelings, to tell me about the first death they can remember. Almost always they can tell me when and who it was. Often it was a significant moment in their lives. We grow and learn to walk, but the first step, if not remembered, still has a lasting significance. Perhaps you can uncover your earliest experience of death and find some way to better handle your present situation.

Anyway, you have to learn to deal with it, not hide it, or avoid it or to try to run away from it. If you do, you might be running all your days. For example, I have noticed some similarities through the years of those who lost a parent when they were quite young, more especially with men who lost their mothers when they were still little boys. Life can be forever colored. It often affects one's ability to trust and give again. If a mother can be taken from a little child who needs her, then anything can happen . . . .Should this be true with you, I suggest you learn to express your feelings toward it, not bury them, not hide them in the cellar . . .or, like the barking dog we used to have at home, he did not go away or quiet down because we decided to close the cellar door. He barked on and on, scratched at the door, annoyed our sleep, awakened the neighbors, made us cranky, and made us wish we had never had a dog at all.

PLEASE SAVE SOME TIME TO LEARN TO GRIEVE

St. Paul wrote, "I have learned, in whatsoever state I am, to be content." That sounds nice. Normally, we use this verse to celebrate his inner peace, no matter what had happened. True, but that is not the message I want to borrow on just now. Concentrate here on the word "learned". Paul did not come by the knowledge naturally, anymore than you or I can speak a foreign language that we have not struggled to learn, nor play the flute the first time we pick it up. It takes work, hard work, learning how to do a new instrument or language, or life.

When it comes to grieving, you and I must learn to do that properly too. It is not as easy as it looks. To learn you will need many different teachers. Others who have walked that road ahead of you will drop back, if you ask them, to tell you what they found along their way. While some find it too painful to do so, most will try to help you. Pastors, parents, teachers, friends will open up your vistas. The Bible can teach you the spiritual lessons for your journey. (At the end of this book we have added a list of relevant Bible passages.) A support group of like-minded people can be of enormous help. A trained counselor can be invaluable. But, it all begins with you, and that is also where it ends.

St. Paul goes on in Philippians 4:13: "I have learned the secret, I can do all things in Christ who strengthens me." That is, it is Jesus Christ who gives me strength. He knew how to grieve himself. He wept. He overcame his fears. He wiped his tears away when he turned it all over to His Heavenly Father. Jesus was a teacher, most of all; after all they called him "Rabbi", which means teacher. You have to learn how to overcome your grief.

Dr. Kubler-Ross and others have conducted endless experiments in ending psychodrama, trying to teach people how to go back and reclaim their grief. They found that some will not let the process happen. They never let it go. The primary purpose of the exercise is to get on with life and leave the grieving to the dead.

Poem

If I should die and leave you here awhile,
Be not like others, soon undone, who keep
Long vigil by the silent dust and weep.
For my sake, turn again to life and smile,
Nerving thy heart and trembling hand to do
Something to comfort weaker hearts than thine.
Complete these dear, unfinished tasks of mine,
And I perchance, may therein comfort you.

ANONYMOUS

• • • •

On the down side, some people cling to grief and use it as a crutch. Some will not surrender it. It gives meaning to their lives. As old men love their illnesses, and young men love their inexperience, some learn to love their grief. It brings them some attention and the concern of others. But that is the wrong lesson. If your life was defined and absorbed by the one who is gone, it will be difficult to find yourself again. If grief lingers on too long, you should seek some help, and then get on with life.

In the old days, dressed in black, the widow paraded through the streets. Armbands were the thing. I remember them. At the time when I was as boy in Pittsburgh, black-ribboned wreaths were still hung on the doors of the homes where the awful thing had struck. Well, thank God we have passed that time; or have we? Have you? Have you managed to get up and go on and out with something else to do and give and think about? Or, have you made your loss the measure of your days? "Slumber not in the tents of your fathers," the Spanish philosopher Unamuno once wrote, "the world is advancing. Advance with it!"

I guarantee you: life will never be the same again. It will all look bleak and dark, more so at the start. But time and the Lord can help you to clear out the clouds. In the end, since God works all things together for good, He will lead you through the Valley, if you allow Him to, and on out to the other side, to the mountain top of your new tomorrow.

Psalm 23 says, "Yea though I walk through the Valley of death, I will fear no evil." Through the valley. Sometimes you need to stir up the gift of God which is within you. The gift is there. Christ promises that. He will never fail you or forsake you. You will need to find it once again. Do not be afraid to say you need help in learning how to grieve. "I have <u>learned</u> to be content." Tough lesson indeed!

3

GRIEF IS AN INDIVIDUAL JOURNEY . . .

These days many authors sell books which document the patterns of human behavior: How to do this and that, including how we should approach illness and death and grief. More especially, they cover what movements in our various passages are predictable. I think they over-simplify the subject. Nothing in grief is predictable. There are no hard and fast patterns. Grief is an individual journey. It is always singular: Your grief or mine. To be sure, I notice some similarities; but human beings seldom fit into molds. You must walk this lonesome valley by yourself. Others can help, of course. They can point you in the prop-er direction; but there is no way to tell another how to journey through grief. I found that the stages we are supposed to go through often over-lap, shift back and forth, and sometimes, do not appear at all.

There is no right way to grieve. No one should try to tell you that there is. There is no wrong way either, except if you try to avoid it. It is futile to try to change the grieving nature of another person. People face grief the way they face everything else, only more so. The quiet person tends to become quieter; the verbal person becomes more talk-ative; the depressive can become more depressed. I say "tends" in all these things, for sometimes it turns the other way around.

As a rule of thumb I advise: "Whatever is, is normal . . ." Whatever is, is normal. (Are you listening?) Do not try to alter normalcy, or try to reshape another into one whose grief will be more agreeable to you.

If a severe problem continues for months and months, it will be time enough to worry about what to do and to seek some help, but at the start grief is largely individual and unpredictable. It is a lonesome valley.

People often try to tell other people how to grieve. I see them getting worried because someone close to them appears to be malfunctioning. He/She either cries too much, or does not cry at all. They feel too guilty or not guilty enough. Sometimes they feel guilty that they do not feel guilty enough. They sleep all the time, or they do not sleep at all . . . As if there were only one right way to do it. Our inability to accept another person's right to individual grief hints at weaknesses within ourselves. We find it difficult to allow another person to be the other person, whether it is a child or parent, an employee or boss, a neighbor, a spouse, a fellow student or teacher. We would rather they become like us.

We want each of them to be the way <u>we</u> are, to be nice to us, to agree with us, thereby to make it easier for us to live and move and have our individual being. When it comes to grief, because we feel we have handled it, or have not; either buried it or passed it on, we would prefer not to be bothered by the weaknesses of others. They mirror the weakness within ourselves; and no one likes that. Their strength can threaten us, or their weakness reminds us of our own.

Even with the most deeply committed Christians: when we decide that everyone in grief needs to declare the same majestic note of faith as we do, in the same majestic words, it can all become naively irreligious. It violates the Scripture's insistence on our individuality. God did not cut us out of identical patterns. He breathed his individual gift of life into each one of us. Each created person is unique. The death of a loved one in the Scripture brings wide varieties of grief. Later in this book I will take you on a little tour of what happens when death occurs in the Bible. There, as here, we find many different attitudes and approaches when it comes to resolving grief, as many as there are people who experience it.

WHAT DEATH CAN NEVER TOUCH,
OR TAKE AWAY . . .

When you lose someone you love, fasten your vision for a few minutes on the things which death can never touch or take away. Death takes a lot away. I don't need to remind anyone who has been there. The whole landscape changes. W. H. Auden caught it essentially in the following poem.

> *Stop all the clocks, cut off the telephone,*
> *Prevent the dog from barking with a juicy bone,*
> *Silence the pianos and with muffled drum*
> *Bring out the coffin, let the mourners come.*
>
> *He was my North, my south, my East and West,*
> *My working week and my Sunday rest,*
> *My noon, my midnight, my talk, my song;*
> *I thought that love would last for ever: I was wrong.*
>
> *The stars are not wanted now: put out every one;*
> *Pack up the moon and dismantle the sun;*
> *Pour away the ocean and sweep up the wood.*
> *For nothing now can ever come to any good.*
>
> . . . .
>
> *O last night I dreamed of you, Johnny, my lover,*

You'd the sun on one arm and the moon on the other,
The sea it was blue and the grass it was green,
Every star rattled a round tambourine;
Ten thousand miles deep in a pit there I lay:
But you frowned like thunder and you went away.

("Two Songs for Hedli Anderson" from <u>Selected Poetry</u>, Second Edition, Vintage Books
W. H. Auden 1971)

• • • •

Each of us loses a lot when a loved one dies. Our souls and psyches
usually go immediately to the things that we have lost. I encourage you
to embrace the things that death can never take away. Death can never
take away your hopes or your dreams of a new tomorrow. Death can
never take away the memories you cherish. The joy of memory is a
priceless treasure. There is a storehouse in your inner being where you
can join hands and walk around with those you have loved and lost
awhile. In the corridors of your mind, you can pick any moment you
wish, and re-live it when you choose. Go back to easier times and better days. Face the photographic albums of your inner self, even when
it is difficult. Go through your letters and the unwritten lists of all the
happy times. As always, remember the good times.

Think of the times that you shared together. Talk about the one who
is gone, how precious he/she was and is. It will make you sad; but then
tears are the price you pay for having loved so much. If you never cared,
you would never feel the loss.

You still have your memories. No one, nothing can ever take them
away. You also have the life that passed from them into others. The
good is not interred with our bones. It lives on, sometimes without visible symbol, as Thucydides the famous Greek philosopher once wrote,
"It is woven into the stuff of other men's lives". He writes:

"So, they received, each for his own memory, praise that grows not
old, and with it the grandest of all sepulchers, not that in which
their mortal bones are laid, but a home in the minds of men, where
their glory remains fresh to stir to speech or action as the occasion
comes by. For the whole earth is the sepulcher of famous men and

women; and their story is not graven only on stone above their native earth, but lives on far away, without visible symbol, woven into the stuff of other people's lives."

THUCYDIDES

Let me not try to deceive you: Death takes away a lot (as if you did not know). It feels like someone turned out all the lights. It takes the color out of things. It throws everything out of focus.

But then it brings everything back into focus, too. It shows you how precious and fleeting are the times we have to be together, how quickly they all pass. The Bible tells us how quickly it goes. Job says time passes like "a weaver's shuttle", click, click, click! The Bible warns us, "You know not what a day may bring forth." It reminds us not to waste the time we have upon the earth in anything but the highest and the best.

• • • •

I spoke with a man not long ago who told me that his father had died several years before in Ireland. He could not afford to go over for the funeral. Eventually, years later, he was finally able to take the trip. He made it to his father's grave. What he told me was amazing. He said that all of a sudden he found himself speaking to his father. He told him things he never knew he knew or felt. For the first time, he said he understood his father and their relationship with each other. He thanked his father for all that he had done, in actual words. He said his father heard him; he was sure of it. Finally he said, "I don't recall all of the details, but a friend was standing right beside me. He heard every word I said." The Bible says, "Though dead, yet he speaketh."

I doubt if we could verify all of that with the Rules of Evidence in "Roberts' Rules of Order". I do not think my friend meant it as literally as those who communicate with the dead in the paranormal world of spiritualism. But, I know that those who are gone can "speak" from beyond the grave. I have spoken to them and listened to them myself.

The last thing that death can never touch is the conviction that life does not end with death. Breathing stops, the body ceases to move, the voice becomes silent, but a new life has begun. You need to learn to believe that.

• • • •

The Book of Hebrews (Chapters 11-12) tells of the "Cloud of Witnesses which looks on," from above. In the Roll Call of The Heroes of the Faith, the author of Hebrews recites a long history of God's Chosen People, all the heroes and how much they gave to be servants of the Lord. Now they are gone, he writes; but they are still here. The "Cloud" is a spatial reference; he did not mean it as a cloud in the sky. He meant that they surround us. In Florida one soon learns that the cloud formations are unique and a source of infinite pleasure for families driving the long road from Jacksonville to parts south, even all the way to Miami. "Hey, do you see a duckie, or a walrus, or Jack Frost?" Do you see?

Wonderful Carlyle Marney, the great Methodist minister from Charlotte and Lake Junaluska, now gone, used to talk about his "balcony people". In a church service for us in Pittsburgh one day, he visualized all of those he had loved and lost awhile, sitting in the balcony. I never enter Southminster Church but that I think about Marney and all the cloud of witnesses we knew.

I look up into my symbolic balcony from time to time, and I think about those who loved me and helped me, and who now from beyond, encourage me to do better. They are watching me, not to note my failures, nor to tell me what I should do. They encourage me to be the best that I can be. Like home team fans in the stands at a World Series or at a Super Bowl Game, they cheer and jump for heavenly joy when my life goes right. They weep when things go wrong. We all can use a fan club. Sometimes people do not feel they have one. But. . .you have one in "the balcony". From up there, all is forgiven; everything is known; everything is new. Those who are gone understand what we long to do and be.

The cloud is always there. Your cloud of witnesses will be a helpful addition to your life. When you see the Florida clouds, pause and ponder whom you see and what they might be saying.

• • • •

A friend called the other day, whose father was quite dear to me, and of course, to him. The father had died. I said, "How are you managing with the loss of your dad?" He said, "Not too well." I asked, "How do you get up when you are down?" He replied, "I try to think of what my father would have done, and what he wants me to do. I can usually feel his presence and 'hear' his voice from up there!" I can hear my Dad and Mother, too.

The wonder is not that we die. The wonder is that we live. The wonder is not that life breaks down in illness and uncertainty, but that it ever builds up to form a living, loving soul. The ultimate in wonder is not death but life, and life which goes on forever more. We get it wrong. We think we own the gift of life. We act as if our hearts keep beating because we tell them to. It takes one sudden death to disabuse you of that notion. Considering all the possibilities and the endless changes through the long and winding evolutionary trail, it is a miracle that we are here at all. Tune in to the presence of those who have left our sight. They can hold you up, when everything and everybody else lets you down.

To make it more personal, I add an incident, which my mother related to me later in her life. A few years before she died she had another serious heart attack. She ended up in a hospital emergency room. Her doctor told me later that she had "died" on the table. Then she experienced one of those widely known "life after life" experiences. She told me that she saw herself floating up from the table. She went through a long and lovely tunnel, surrounded by a bright shining light. She came out the other side, and there she saw her father, her mother, her two brothers, her grandparents, and endless friends, all of whom were gone. Not one person she "saw" there was still alive on earth. She said it was a joyful time. She felt so peaceful.

But, next she heard her doctor saying, "Margaret, breathe now... breathe, breathe." She did not like his voice, not at that moment anyway. Medical assistants were pounding on her chest. Before long, she witnessed her own spiritual body receding back down through the tunnel and floating down to the emergency room table to rejoin the body she had so recently left.

It is puzzling, I know. I do not know how you manage to absorb that kind of story, I know what she said she felt. She concluded, "Richard, it was so wonderful! I will never fear death again. They are all waiting for me." I will never fear death either; and neither should you. Life does not end with what we call death!

CHRIST WILL SEE YOU THROUGH. . .

A verse in Psalm 23 says ". . .Though I walk through the valley of the shadow of death, I will fear no evil." The valley comes, but you will never have to walk through it alone. Christ will see you through the valley. John 14 can help you with the dark and dreary moments of your days. Knowing that His hour had come to leave, Jesus gave his disciples a vision of what would happen after He was taken away. He was troubled by the thought of His coming death, and the impending betrayal of His friends. He went into His private garden to pray, to turn it all over to the Father. While he was there, the disciples he left behind to keep watch fell asleep. He scolded them, but He understood how tired they were.

Next, He reassured them that the world still belonged to Him. It still would be redeemed by Him. He promised them that He would remain with them forever with the gift of the Holy Spirit, the Comforter, "Whom the Father will send in my name. . ." Meanwhile, "I will not leave you comfortless; I will come to you." Indeed.

Catch the grandeur of those words. Take them with you as you go. Let them lighten up your darkest valleys. Share them with your neighbors and your family near and far away. Whisper them to your deepest doubts and highest hopes. Take them with you when you wonder why on earth the world is made in such a way that human hearts can ache and break and fly to pieces in a sad and terribly unwanted moment. Repeat them when you stand bewildered before the news you never thought you would have to hear.

Those words are a gift of Christ to you. "Let not your hearts be troubled, neither let them be afraid." You need them, however strong and bold and powerful you try to appear to be, or of how you seem to be to other people in your world. Jesus said: "I will not leave you comfortless." The Lord God knows your frame. He knows how frail we really are.

Other comforts may desert you. Other kingdoms rise and fall. Other promises are broken. But, in whatever discomfort you might find your self today, or any day, years ago or years to come, decades even... in every case, listen to the words: "I will not leave you comfortless; I will come to you", as reassuring as a friend or father who says in your time of crisis, "Don't worry, hold on, I will be there soon."

• • • •

It is as if you were a little child, alone in the darkness of the night: "I'm afraid, Mom," the little girl said, "I don't want to be there in my room alone." "Why?" "Because I'm scared there by myself," she said, "that's why." A parent being beside you in the dark does not really change a thing. Whatever evil lurked behind the shadows, or the things that go "bump" in the night, remain. But still, it helps to have someone to hold your hand. We can usually stand the darkness if someone is there to walk us through it. "I just needed to hear your voice," he said. Or, "Please come over for a minute, then I'll be okay". . . You can smile until you cry. It is so tender, but so strong and final.

To be alone is the fear we feel. "Oh, please don't leave me", he pleaded when his wife had died. I stayed with him, all that night. He said ever after that, that he never would have made it without my presence. Loneliness is the other name of many other problems in our lives. Like Solzhenitsyn told us in the Gulag Archipelago: "They didn't have to torture us in the Russian prison camp. . .all they had to do was lock us up in a dark and empty room alone. . . then, on being released, we were ready to do anything not to have to go back. We were so terrified of being alone in the darkness. The happiest day of all my life", he continued, "was the day they put me in a prison cell with another person." He was not yet free, but he was no longer alone. Something deep within us is severely damaged when we have no one to share the pain. It is worse when it comes to the loss of one we loved. Jesus died alone; but because of Him, you and I will never have to. He promises to be there in the one last pilgrimage that each must make alone.

My old professor of homiletics loved to tell the story of the little girl who was reassured by her mother that God was with her there in her bedroom when she tried to go to sleep each night. "Oh, I know that", little Ivy said, "but I want a God with skin on his face!" Indeed, the God Incarnate.

• • • •

Just when you cannot take another moment, look up, hold out your hand.... Christ will be there to take it. Christ will see you through.... At your darkest moments He will not go ahead or follow you. He will be by your side and where you need him to, He will carry you. I often think about "Footprints":

One night a man had a dream.
He dreamed he was walking along the beach with the Lord.
Across the sky flashed scenes from his life.
For each scene, he noticed two sets of footprints in the sand:
One belonging to him, and the other to the Lord.

When the last scene of his life flashed before him, he looked back at the footprints in the sand. He noticed that many times along the path of his life there was only one set of footprints. He also noticed that it happened at the very lowest and saddest times in his life.

This really bothered him and he questioned the Lord about it. "Lord, You said that once I decided to follow You, You'd walk with me all the way. But I have noticed that during the most troublesome times in my life, there is only one set of footprints. I don't understand why when I needed You most You would leave me."

The Lord replied, "My son, My precious child, I love you and would never leave you. During your times of trial and suffering, when you see only one set of footprints, it was then that I carried you."

Author unknown

• • • •

The word "comfortless" can be translated into a lot of different English words: "I will not leave you desolate", The Revised Standard Version reads. "I will not abandon you," The Living Bible says. The Good News For Modern Man reads: "When I go, you will not be left alone." My favorite is The King James original translation: "I will not leave you comfortless." One of the softest and most reassuring promises in the entire world: "I will comfort you." With no one to "comfort" you, you will really be done! Comfort is one of my most favorite words in all the English language.

Literally, comfortless comes from the Greek "orphanos", which means, and you will catch the transliteration, "I will not leave you as orphans." One translation says, "I will not leave you as orphans in the storm." The classical Greek is broader. When Plato was relating the feelings of the disciples after Socrates was executed, he wrote that they were all <u>orphanos</u>, like orphans: helpless, comfortless, abandoned. . . . What a pity. The promise of Jesus was/is that we will never be orphans, never be without comfort. He will always be there. And, He will send "The Comforter" to be there too.

We are each and all in need of comfort, no matter how strong and proud we think we are, or how self sufficient we pretend to be. We all need tenderness. The biggest grouch you know needs kindness, even if he does not know it, or admit it. Each of us needs understanding: parents and their children, children and their parents, husbands and their wives, wives and their husbands, friend to friend to everyone: all of us need comfort.

I promise you there is One who will give it to you. There is One who stands and waits beside your grief at the end of every day, One who greets you every morning alongside the awful empty feeling that it is true. A woman left alone told me once that mornings are worse than evenings. I had never thought about it that way. "Why?", I asked. She said, "Because it is true all over again." Christ will be there to greet you. God Almighty waits at the top of every morning and at the top of every hill, and in every valley too; when, stumbling, tired or broken, you finally head for home. He is there waiting for you, to welcome you, to reassure you that life is more than now, that it will all work out for good.

Meanwhile, Jesus says, "When You Lose Someone You Love", the road is rugged, long and steep, often lonely and alone. Sometimes, the clouds dip down to touch the earth so that you can barely see your way ahead. . .lost and afraid, deafened by the noise, you must listen one more time, Jesus Christ is speaking. . .perhaps to you. . . "Fear not, I will be with you. Be of good cheer. I have overcome the world." I will come to you and give you everything you need. Christ will see you through.

Near the end of the Bible we read these words: "I saw a new heaven and a new earth. The first heaven and the first earth were passed away; and there was no more sea. And I John saw the holy city, new Jerusalem, coming down from God out of heaven, prepared as a bride adorned for her husband. And I heard a great voice out of heaven saying, Behold, the tabernacle of God is with men, and He will dwell with them, and they shall be His people, and God Himself shall be with them, and be their God. And God shall wipe away all tears from their eyes; and there shall be no more death, neither sorrow, nor crying, neither shall there be any more pain, for the former things are passed away."

• • • •

"And there shall be no more curse; but the throne of God and the Lamb shall be in it; and His servants shall serve Him; and they shall see His face; and His name shall be in their foreheads. And there shall be no night there; and they need no candle, neither light of the sun; for the Lord God giveth them light; and they shall reign for ever and ever."

(REVELATION 21, 22)

PART II

THE BIBLE DEALS WITH DEATH

INTRODUCTION

THE BACKGROUND FROM THE SCRIPTURE

Most believing Christians try to look to the Bible for help, but sometimes they do not know where to turn. There are additional insights available from other books, from psychologists, grief therapists, teachers, and ministers; but I offer this brief summary of how the stories of the Scripture can be useful to you when you lose someone you love. They are meditative and spiritual. In this section we look in on the day-by-day experiences of God's people and how they responded when death came to someone they loved.

DEATH OF A SPOUSE

"Jacob Journeyed On. . ."

Oh how Jacob loved Rachel! She was the apple of his eye. He worked and waited seven years plus seven more, before her father Laban would allow him to marry her. But it was worth it. "The years seemed but a few days", the Bible says, "because of the love he had for her." They finally married. He was filled with joy. . . . Not that life was easy. They had more than their share of troubles. Later, one son, Joseph, was sold into slavery by his own brothers. That ended happily, but oh the tears in Jacob's eyes when he was told that Joseph was gone. (Genesis 35)

Jacob became lame and remained a cripple for the rest of his life. His daughter Dinah was raped by a foreigner. Her brothers, Simeon and Levi, took outrageous revenge, embarrassing their father. Along the way, some of his twelve sons (ten of them by his first wife, Leah) lost their faith. That upset their father more than any of his other disappointments. They married foreign, non-believing wives. That broke Jacob's heart. Then, their "Nanny", kind old Deborah, died. They buried her under an oak tree in Bethel. Their life was moving on, and on, and on. . . . . This couple never had it easy. But Jacob and Rachel faced it all together, and that doubled their strength.

Then one day, it reads, "They journeyed on from Bethel". "When they came near Ephrath (which we know as Bethlehem), Rachel's days were accomplished that she should be delivered. . .and she brought forth her second-born son." How nice to have a baby in Bethlehem. Echo Mary. Echo Joseph. Echo everybody. . .a boy child in Bethlehem. What else could a couple want? But. . .it was not an easy birth: "She travailed, and had hard labor. . ." The midwife reassured her, "Fear not, you will have another son."

But alas, things got worse. Rachel was in trouble: moments of agony at the moment of her ecstasy. "Her soul was departing", it says, right at the crowning moment of the birth of her new child and she was a young woman. "Rachel". . .the Bible then whispers. . "died in child-birth", at Bethlehem. "Oh, goodness, no!" Jacob shouted. "Why did that have to happen, Lord? Why to me? Why to her? Why now?"

A lot of other things followed, but all the Bible adds is, "He buried her outside the town of Bethlehem (Old Testament people always buried before the next sundown). And, he set a pillar upon her grave, which is there to this day". Rachel's tomb is still there. I saw it myself, in Bethlehem, a couple of years ago. Israeli soldiers guard it closely.

The Book of Genesis, however, is impatient to get on with the story of what God is about to do with Jacob and his sons. No time to linger here on Jacob's grief. It adds with solemn finality: "Jacob journeyed on and he pitched his tent beyond the Tower of Edar." What a pity. Rachel was buried. . .and Jacob journeyed on, a lonely awful journey.

His grief was the price he paid for loving her. That's why it hurt him; he loved her. Five million people die in our world, each and every day. That is an awesome number. But the one death, which cuts you or me in two, is the death of the one we love too much to lose.

So much was gone. . . . His hurt was deep. . . . But, ask Jacob, even in the loneliest of all his moments when the midwife frantically came to bring the news of Rachel's death: "Jacob, would you exchange the love you had for Rachel through the years for a lessening of your pain just now?" (Like crossing the River Styx, to forget his pain, Charon said, "You must forget the pleasure, too.") Jacob would say, "No thanks. Of course not! I loved her then. I love her now. I will always love her. I would marry her again in a minute. I will keep my memories safe and secure, forever."

• • • •

"Why did it have to happen?" Why? Do not be afraid to ask that mighty one-word question. "I know you are not supposed to ask 'why'," the little widow whispered to me years ago. "Why not?" I said, "Why not ask the question 'Why'?" The prophets often did. Job asked God why. Jeremiah questioned God right to his face. Jesus peered up into the heavens from the Cross and cried out, "Why Father, why hast Thou forsaken me?" If God is God, there must be an answer, even when we cannot find it.

You are allowed to ask, but once you do, you must accept the given answer. And, it is often not as mysterious or as ethereal as we want to make it. It all comes down to this: We die because we live. If grief is the price you pay for loving, then death is the price you pay for living. Nothing, no one, lasts forever. Only God, and His Eternal Presence in Jesus Christ were there at the beginning and only He will be there at the end.

There are mysteries to be sure, but I think the proper phrasing of the question is not "Why?" but "Why now?" Why not in some other circumstance? Why not ten or twenty years from now? Why not more peacefully and more calmly? No one asks why a ninety-seven-year-old woman dies in her sleep.

Young Rachel's poor little weakened body could not stand it anymore. God did not punish her with an early death. She was made and lived in such a way that under such stress and intrusion, her body could tolerate it no longer. Human life is fragile. As I mentioned earlier: The wonder is not that we die, but that we live. The ultimate in wonder is not death, but life.

"Jacob journeyed on." A mighty sentence. I offer it to you for your marching orders if you have lost your spouse. He journeyed on, not because he wanted to. . .(Tell the truth Jacob, wouldn't you just as soon be buried there beside her. . . at the beginning, anyway?) . . .not because he wanted to, but because he had to. He had their family to rear. There was the new little baby boy, Benjamin, and the eleven larger boys, and the little girls and the larger girls. Beyond the family, there was the family of man. Other lives had need of Jacob. God needed him as well, to keep the Biblical story going on and on and on.

Our God is a God of the future. He will not allow us to dwell in the memories of yesteryear. He commands us to get up and pitch our tents toward Edar. God only knows where Edar was. This is the only mention of the little towered town. But it meant that God was moving Jacob to the future. You too must journey on, because if you refuse, you will deny the presence and the power of The Heavenly Father! That is what Jesus meant when he said what sounds so unsympathetic: "Let the dead bury the dead. Come and follow me." Otherwise, you carry the burden of the past. You will live with and for the ghosts. The dead depend upon the living to carry on their lives, but the verb is carry-on, Jacob journeyed on. . . .

KING DAVID AND HIS SAD TIMES. . .

David had his good times, even great times. Gifted with extraordinary skill and sensitivity, he was secretly anointed by Samuel to become the future King of Israel while he was still a boy in Jesse's house. Before he was fully grown, he volunteered to fight the mighty Goliath, and he won the battle with a stone from his slingshot. He later won his military battles. He danced up and down the streets of Jerusalem when he was coroneted King. He lived a good long life as the greatest monarch in the history of his nation. No one is more revered in Israel than King David! George Washington, Abraham Lincoln, and Thomas Jefferson all rolled into one. But, he had his other moments, days and months, and years, especially when he lost people that he loved. Let me tell you of a few of them and see what we can learn:

The Death Of a Friend. . .

The first time David faced the death of one he loved was the passing of his best friend, Jonathan. David was still a young man. Jonathan and he had knitted a friendship so deep and strong that some have even speculated how close they might have been. They enjoyed each other, they confided in each other, they protected each other, and they loved each other. You are lucky if you have a friend like Jonathan, or David.

But, in a poorly waged battle, led by his failing father King Saul, which ended with Saul's suicide, Jonathan was killed by the conquering

Philistines. When they brought the news to David, he was crushed and broken. He "rent his clothes", a Biblical expression of deep grief. He mourned and fasted, he cried and carried on. In a little while he wrote a personal lamentation for his departed friend. His tribute is in I Samuel Chapter One:

"David and Jonathan, beloved and lovely!
In life and in death they were not divided,
They were swifter than eagles,
They were stronger than lions.
. . .

I am distressed for you, my brother Jonathan;
Very pleasant you have been to me;
Your love to me was wonderful,
Passing the love of women.
How are the mighty fallen. . ."

It helped David to write some words for his friend. I find it usually helps to write your memories when you lose someone you love. I have read and listened to countless personal tributes at memorial services through the decades. I almost always encourage people to write down some thoughts of the deceased. I ask young children to do it, especially grandchildren. Time passes. The recollections of a particular friend, or loved one, or grandparent, can blend together and recede through the years; but a written diary or poem or sketch will last forever.

The story of another's life often gives meaning to the death. It does not have to be fine and excellent prose or poetry, just a personal, private memory. In the Old Testament, if you were remembered, you were not gone from the earth. Sit down and start. You will be grateful later on. David never forgot Jonathan, and we still have his poetic tribute.

But life moved along. Jonathan left behind a crippled five-year-old son named Mephibosheth (II Samuel 4:4). After his friend died, David took care of Jonathan's son. In time he called him to his court and showed him kindness, "for his father's sake". David even gave some of Saul's land to Mephibosheth. He took care of him for the rest of his life.

That is a grand part of the story. It helps to be able to take care of the family or the children of the one you lose. Step out with courage to set your grief aside by promising to be good to those family members who remain. We can honor the deceased and temper our own loss if we reach out to heal and help those who remain.

• • • •

The Death Of David's Child

The second time David experienced the death of a loved one was the sad, sad moment when his infant son died. There is a puzzling background to the story, but we want to focus on what David did when the child was ill and after he died.

When it became clear that the infant was in trouble (II Samuel 12:16), "David besought God for the child". He fasted and lay prostrate all night long. He prayed and prayed. His servants tried to get him to eat, but he refused for seven long days and nights. If you have ever been forced to watch and wait for news of a child in trouble, you know exactly how he felt. He fasted and worried and prayed and wept. But the child died anyway.

When it happened, the servants were afraid to tell the King, remembering that he was so distraught while the boy was still alive. They feared what he would do now that the boy was gone. David saw them whispering. He knew. He asked, "Is the child dead?" "He is dead," they replied.

Then watch what happened next. . ."David arose from the earth and washed and anointed himself, and changed his clothes; he went into the house of the Lord; and worshipped, and when they set food before him, he ate."

The servants were dumbfounded: "How can this be?" David answered, "While the child was still alive, I fasted and wept; for I said, 'Who knows whether the Lord will be gracious to me, that the child may live?' But now that he is dead, why should I fast? Can I bring him back again? No, I shall go to him, but he will not return to me." (II Samuel 12:22-23)

The passage is quite helpful, not only following an infant's death. Notice that it cut David to the heart when his son was critically ill. It always does. It is against the laws of nature and of human compassion for a parent to lose a child. One's helplessness prompts all kinds of fasting and bargaining and prayers. "Oh dear, please no, Lord, do not take my child." It is especially devastating to watch the deterioration and death of a small child: gone before life ever gave its chances and its joys. A parent never forgets. "Please, Lord, please." "When you lose a parent you lose the past", a friend of mine wrote, "when you lose a child, you lose the future."

David and Bathsheba's son died anyway. They lost their child before his life got underway. David surprised his servants. They expected him to collapse completely. But he rose and went back to work. How? He tells you. While my son was alive there was some hope that God might heal him. After the boy was gone there was nothing more to do. It was time to say goodbye. That is just the way life is. It is not always fair. God lost his only son to a horrible death on a cross; other fathers and mothers do, too. "I shall go to him, he will not return to me." It is time to turn the page.

David had a choice to make: either throw his life and kingdom and family and marriage on the rocks and wallow in self-pity, or he could be strong and show himself to be a Man of God. One day he would go on to meet the boy. Although a tear formed in the corner of his eye now and then, and while he wondered why this happened to him, and while he grudgingly looked back over his shoulder, he went on to live his life.

It says that he comforted Bathsheba, his wife, the mother of the child. I am grateful the author included that. Individual parents can be selfish when a child dies. Sometimes they cannot help it. One intensive study discovered that nine out of ten marriages were severely shaken with the death of a child. Sometimes an individual can dwell on individual grief and forget about the partner. I have seen it many times.

I try to understand the pressures, how a father particularly will try to carry the burden of grief for the whole family. Then he collapses too, and great is the fall. Take time to grieve. David comforted his wife, and out of that togetherness, she conceived another son, whom David called Solomon. Solomon, as you know, became the successor to his father. The Bible stories almost all have happy endings.

If you have lost a child, I encourage you to seek help from those who have been through it. The longest road of all is the road home from the funeral of a son or daughter. In many parts of the country there are support groups called "Compassionate Friends". In other areas they have other names. Members gather to help each other and to find the strength they need. Do not try to make it on your own.

• • • •

The Death Of A Grown Son

The third time King David experienced the death of one he loved was the untimely death of his warrior son named Absalom. We sometimes forget the pain of aging parents when their older children die. In the second year of my ministry I went to call on an eighty-six-year-old mother whose sixty-four-year-old son had died suddenly. Sixty-four seemed a ripe old age to me, back then when I was twenty-six. But I missed it. She was as sad as a thirty-year-old mother I met the following year whose six-year-old had been killed in an auto accident. Parenthood does not change with age. He was her son.

In David's case, you would think that the death of Absalom (II Samuel 18:24-33) would have been a great relief. Absalom became confused. Many children do. They say and do things which would be better undone. Absalom led an armed rebellion against his father's kingdom. Twenty thousand men lost their lives in the ensuing battle. Finally, Absalom lost his life, too. A messenger was sent to tell the king.

"David was sitting between the two gates", it says, "when the messenger came running up to the palace." Ahimaaz, the runner, called out "All is well," and he bowed before King David. Ahimaaz meant that the rebellion had been squelched! David's first question was: "Is it well with my son Absalom?" . . .The Cushite was puzzled, but in a little while he reassured the King, "May all who rise up against you be as dead as Absalom."

Then, it says, "The King was deeply moved, and went up to his chamber and wept. He said, "My son Absalom, my son, my son Absalom! Would God that I had died instead of you. Oh Absalom, my son, my son!" Every grieving parent knows the feeling. "What could I have done to make his life easier? Oh God, how I wish it had been me."

Joab, David's Chief of Staff, scolded the King. "Your men fought for you, they won, and still you weep for Absalom. I perceive that if Absalom were alive and all of us were dead today, you would be pleased." (II Samuel 19:6) Well, Joab had his reasons, but his words to the king no doubt were appropriate. He was thinking of the Kingdom. But David knew that compared to the death of a son, even a rebellious and defiant one, nothing else in the world will do. Kingdoms rise and fall. A lost child is lost forever.

David ascended to the throne again, but, he never forgot Absalom. It does not say, but I have always felt, that David kept wondering what he had done to drive his son away. Most parents feel puzzlement and guilt when their children turn against them. It is not an easy feeling to chase away, especially if the child dies while you are estranged. David's problems got worse from then on, but the hardest moment of his latter years was the death of Absalom, his son.

• • • •

David's Final Words

The last death David faced, as with every one of us, was his own. II Kings 2 tells the story. David's time to go had come, "He charged Solomon his son, saying, 'I am about to go the way of all the earth. Be strong and show yourself a man, and keep the charge of the Lord your God, walking in His ways and keeping His statutes. . . If you and your sons take heed to their way, to walk in faithfulness with all their heart, and with all their soul, there shall not fail you a man on the throne of Israel.'"

Most of them failed to listen as the years rolled on. But the promise and the warning remained forever true. I think every father, and mother, too, should tell their children what they want and expect from them, not in a punitive way, but openly and honestly. Jacob called his twelve sons in Genesis 49:2: "Gather yourselves together, that I may tell you what shall befall you in the days to come." Each son received an individual message, and blessing. David did the same with Solomon. Whether Solomon and his successors listened, was up to them.

I encourage parents to be brave and kind enough to write down some expectations of what is good and holy for their children and grandchildren to follow. It need not be too detailed, but it should be a statement, as David and Jacob made, of what the following generation should revere and try to emulate. "This is what I stood for" is the primary message. "Here is what mattered to me." "Live to make me proud."

The Loss of a Daughter . . .

(Mark 5)

Jairus was an important ruler of the ancient Synagogue. When he spoke, people listened. He was good and wise. He had everything; but everything is not enough when family troubles come. One day his beloved little daughter became ill. "She is to the point of death", he said, as he pleaded with Jesus to come with him to his house to heal her. Jesus went. On the way, the news came that his little girl had died. Sad, sad day for Jairus. Some standing by told him not to bother Jesus. "It is too late!" Jesus said, "Do not fear, only believe."

When they got there, a grieving crowd of family and neighbors had gathered at the house. They were weeping and wailing. Nothing touches a community as deeply as the death of a young person. It hurts everybody. Jesus spoke to them: "Why do you weep?" He asked. "The little girl is not dead, she is sleeping." Mark writes that they laughed at him, so absurd was his statement.

Then, Jesus led Jairus and his wife inside the house and into the little girl's room. Taking her hand, Jesus said (in Aramaic) "Talitha cumi", which means, "Little girl, arise." Immediately she got up and walked. "All around were amazed." No wonder!

What a fantastic story! I have always loved it. It helps so much, even if a problem arises when our children die and Jesus does not come by to bring them back to life on earth. In spite of our prayers and pleas and promises, some children are taken from us too soon. Is there anything to update the story to our time, to give it power when you lose a daughter or son you love? I think there is….

The words of Jesus: "Talitha cumi", offer most of what we need. We probably will not see the literal miracle He performed when the child came back to life. But, "Little girl (Little boy), arise" is the most comforting promise I have ever found. They are not dead, but sleeping.

It will take a while, "He will not return to me", David said, "but I shall go to him." One day, when a thousand years have passed as a watch in the night, when every thing and every one else is over and gone, Christ will still be there. He was there at the beginning. He will be there at the end. To your son or daughter, He will say again, "Talitha cumi"; and the child will rise to live forevermore.

Life can be awful sometimes. Death should not come to children. But when it does, pass on the comforting story of the day that the daughter of Jairus got up and walked away. Glory be to God! Christ is Lord of life and death. Our children in Christ and we ourselves will rise and live for evermore. Believe that we will all be together again, and everything we now know in part, we will then understand in full.

THE DEATH OF A BROTHER OR SISTER

"Families are funny", my uncle Bill Acker used to say, "You never know what anybody is going to say or do." Tolstoy said it more formally: "All happy families are the same. Each unhappy family is unhappy in its own way." Some families, most I would guess, are both: happy and unhappy, interwoven, mixed, individual. But unpredictable things happen. My friend in St. Andrews, Scotland says, "That's just family. That's all there is to it!"

Throughout the Scripture, there is a most uneven, at times even hostile relationship between siblings. It appeared as the first two brothers became embroiled in a dreadful fight. "Cain rose up against his brother Abel, and killed him. The Lord said to Cain, 'Where is Abel your brother?' He said, 'I do not know: Am I my brother's keeper?'" (Genesis 4:8-9) The Lord replied, "Yes you are! The voice of your brother's blood is crying to me from the ground."

Now that is not what you would expect in a sacred story of brotherly relationships, least of all in the first family created by God. It does not mention what the parents, Adam and Eve, said or felt about it. But you can be sure it was a dreadful burden for them.

• • • •

I mentioned that my little brother Bobby died suddenly when he was barely forty-three. My Dad went silent at the time and never really recovered. My mother cried (of course) and said she wished she could have died in his place. It is against the laws of nature and life that a child should die before a parent. But, they often do.

But, to go back to sibling relationships in the Bible, we see more negative than positive. Jacob and Esau, e.g., were in a strained relationship that lasted for almost a lifetime. They were twins. That casts a longer shadow on their love. My dad was an identical twin who had a special love for his brother Howard. The latter died when they were sixty-eight or so. I was young, but I remember how it was a special burden for my father.

Jacob, with his mother's help, swindled his brother Esau out of the family fortune. Esau was the elder twin and thereby entitled to the birthright inheritance from Isaac their father. But Rebekah loved Jacob more (Is there always a "favorite" son or daughter of the parents in a family?). She arranged for the boy to steal the blessing, deceived poor aging Isaac, whose eyes had grown dim. The Bible is so honest about human faults and foibles, all the games we play, and how family works.

Leah and Rachel, sisters, daughters of Laban, had their problems too. They were both married to the same husband, Jacob, at the same time Leah had ten sons with him (no one bothers to say how many daughters). Rachel, the favorite wife of Jacob, came along later. The last two of the twelve sons of Jacob were born to her: Joseph and Benjamin.

• • • •

In the time of Jacob's children it did not improve. Joseph's brothers were jealous: no wonder, the way his father treated him and the way Joseph verbally lorded it over them. They were so jealous they decided to kill Joseph. Instead they sold him to the Midianite traders who sold him into slavery in Egypt. The story had a happy ending in the Salvation of Jacob-Israel's family, but there was huge enmity among the children. It could be that it was because they were half brothers. That can be the root of some of the trouble; but it was a worry to their father.

We cover the death of some of David's children in another part of this book. Here we are calling attention to the sibling rivalries and rebellion in his family. Lawless rebellion brought warfare between father and sons and brothers. It almost destroyed King David.

You do not have to linger long with the sons of King David to realize his was what we call a dysfunctional family. I wonder why. David was the youngest of eight brothers. The youngest son (or daughter) almost always has a special role. The middle child syndrome is legendary. The "baby child" carries some special privileges, but also it has some special burdens. The eldest children have theirs as well.

David's mother, almost never mentioned, is, thankfully remembered for her godliness (Psalm 86:16). His father Jesse was a poor shepherd in Bethlehem. Their humble position in life is mentioned by the prophets Micah (5:2) and Isaiah (11:1). In that modest home, a Godly woman did her best.

• • • •

In the New Testament, it does not improve. It says in Luke 15, "a certain man had two sons." The parable of the prodigal son goes on to tell us that the boys were different. They were jealous of each other, or at least the Elder was jealous of the younger. When the father threw a grand party to celebrate the return of the younger son, the elder brother refused to attend. It hurt the father that his son did not care to rejoice on his brother's return from a far country: "He was dead and now is alive again. He was lost and now is found." The Elder brother was suspicious.

Simon Peter and Andrew were brothers. Jesus chose two sets of brothers to be part of the twelve, the other two were twins: James and John. Andrew met Jesus first. He was the younger brother. When he persuaded Peter to go and talk to Jesus, the later took over and became the chief of the disciples. It does not say what Andrew felt about being over-shadowed by his big brother, but you can be sure, he noticed it.

With our Lord and His own brothers there was trouble throughout His life. They thought He was crazy and that He should cease and desist from claiming to be the Messiah. Later, after His death and resurrection, they seem to have become apostles, especially James who led the Jerusalem Church for twenty years. But He too knew what it was like to face tension and jealousy in the home.

• • • •

Now not all families or twins or brothers and sisters experience difficulties, not in the Bible and surely not ever since. I mention those only to ease our way into the topic of losing a brother or sister to death when the relationship has not been perfect. The sisters Mary and Martha were different. The one was a free spirit (Mary). She preferred to think and laugh and enjoy life, especially with Jesus. She sat down at his feet to adore him. Meanwhile, in one incident, Martha was left with the chores of cleaning up the house and preparing the meal and setting the table. I think it was in her personality. She couldn't let herself go to relax and enjoy the company. She complained to Jesus. He scolded her (mildly). "Come on Martha, relax and enjoy the visit." Why is it that children of the same parents, reared and raised in the same home with the same discipline, and identical rules, and with the same genes turn out differently?

Another day, later on, the girls' brother Lazarus died. (John 11) Notice that this time it is good old dependable Martha who went out to find Jesus, or who was on her way anyway when she met him. It says, "Mary sat in the house." Her grief was uncontrollable. Some siblings fall to pieces at the death of a brother or sisters. Others carry on. Martha said to Jesus, "If you had been here, our brother would not have died." I remember feeling a touch of that on the morning I found my brother Bobby. "Oh Lord, if you had been here, he would still be alive." I knew better, but my feelings reminded me of Martha. It is not easy to say goodbye to a brother or a sister whom you love.

Martha then told Mary that Jesus had come: "The teacher is here," she said, "and He is calling for you." She rose quickly and went to him. Mary fell at his feet. Then, in the shortest verse in the Bible, it says, "Jesus wept." Even though he knew he would raise Lazarus from the dead in just a little while, Jesus was sorry that their brother, his friend, had died. He wept.

It is all right to cry when your brother or sister dies. If you did not love you would have to not mourn. After all, you shared a lifetime of memories and hopes and dreams and secrets together, however long or short it was, you grew up together. No one other than your parents, if you still have them, has known you longer than your brother or sister. No one knows more about you or would miss you more. Wordsworth in one of his earliest poems wrote that he hoped that when he was old, he would still remember how it was when he was young. So do we all.

> *Dear native regions, I foretell,*
> *From what I feel at this farewell,*
> *That, wheresoe'er my steps shall tend,*
> *And whensoe'er my course shall end,*
> *If in that hour a single tie*
> *Survive of local sympathy,*
> *My soul will cast the backward view,*
> *The longing look alone on you.*
>
> *Thus, while the Sun sinks down to rest*
> *Far in the regions of the west,*
> *Though to the vale no parting beam*
> *Be given, not one memorial gleam,*
> *A lingering light he fondly throws*
> *On the dear hills where first he rose.*
>
> WILLIAM WORDSWORTH

• • • •

Years ago James Agee wrote a book called "A Death in the Family." It was a masterpiece. It delved into the strain put on a family when a beloved family member dies. Grief is a mighty power always; it reaches deeper and further when your sister or brother dies.

I have mentioned that when my brother died suddenly in Mt. Lebanon, Pennsylvania, it shook me to the core. He was my pal, my fellow traveler, the best man at my wedding, closer than my closest friends could ever be. One day when he was a little child, I went out at night alone to find him when he was lost. When anyone picked on him, they picked on me too. I introduced him to our neighborhood games and softened his initiations into our clubs.

When we were growing up we shared an old attic room in the East End of Pittsburgh, on Garfield Hill. In the summer it was hot up there. When those huge Bermuda Highs hung around Western Pennsylvania, no one could breathe, let alone sleep, in a third floor attic. Old people literally prayed for their lives. Young people like us, threw ice water on each other in our beds, without notice of course! And, when we ran out of water, we threw other things as well. We lived a special separate life, apart from our parents and our two sisters who slept more comfortably down on the second floor. We shared a pile of baseball cards from the 1950's. We always argued which ones belonged to whom all the way up to when Bobby died. If he were here I would give him all the cards. All the fun, if not the value of the cards, is gone away. I still have them.

• • • •

I also remember when my mother's eldest sister Kathryn died. She was the first to go in Mom's family. Then her favorite brother Conrad died suddenly at 56, then Uncle Pete at 48, then Millie out in Texas, their finally Uncle Bill. Each death tore a chunk out of my Mother's heart and soul. When you bury a sibling, brother or sister, you put a lot of yourself into the ground. It does not matter what you believe is the ultimate destination of the soul and everlasting glory. It is comforting to know they are with the Lord. But, I always say, "If my wife or one of our children or grandchildren were going to glorious Hawaii to bask in eternal sun forever more, I still would weep if I knew that they were never-ever coming back."

I treasure the verses in John 14 where Jesus says, "I go to prepare a place for you, and if I go I will come again…that where I am there you will be also." I believe those comforting words. "Let not your heart be troubled." But…I still would rather have my brother here with me.

There are times when illness and suffering can become so severe that my previous statement would be reversed. I would gladly surrender one I loved in great pain to the Lord of Heaven to find peace in that place where there is no sorrow or suffering or darkness at all. But Bobby was fine when he went to sleep; only he did not wake up the next morning. I don't worry where he is; I only miss him while he is gone.

So, when you lose a sister or brother, part of you is lost too. You grow up together. You laugh, scheme, cry and dream together. Most siblings have family, personal nicknames for each other. They stick.

Up on Cape Cod, near Falmouth, I came across a favorite local poem. I leave you with it now:

WHEN I SAIL AWAY

Sometime at eve when the tide is low,
I shall slip my moorings and sail away,
With no response to the friendly hail
Of kindred craft in the busy bay –
In the silent hush of the twilight pale.
When the night stoops down to embrace the day
And the voices call o'er the waters flow –
Sometime at evening when the tide is low
I shall slip my moorings and sail away.

....

A few who have watched me sail away
Will miss my craft from the busy bay,
Some friendly barks that were anchored near,
Some loving hearts that my soul held dear,
In silent sorrow shall drop a tear.
But I shall have peacefully furled my sail
In moorings sheltered from storm and gale
And greeted friends who have sailed before
O'er the Unknown sea to the Well Known Shore.

10

SUDDEN DEATH

"When Enoch Walked With God. . ."

The Bible tells of several sudden deaths, most of which are the result of warfare or instant punishment. Strange and mysterious episodes are reported where hundreds, thousands, even tens of thousands fall instantly. I leave those to your imaginings.

The Bible knows how startling a sudden death can be, as well as the peculiar set of bewildering feelings that accompany it. "He was there one moment and the next he was gone", the farmer's son told me, "I felt so helpless." Another said, "I waved goodbye when he left for work in the morning. I never saw him again. I keep thinking he'll come back."

We feel helpless in the mystery of life's ending. No death of a loved one is easy, but a sudden termination is a particular burden. Human life is fragile. Saying goodbye is difficult. But it is worse when you cannot say goodbye at all.

The lack of preparation aggravates the problem. A long terminal illness is filled with pain and fear and regret, but at least, if you are wise, it gives you time to tidy it all up and tie your lives together. Words can be spoken, promises offered, and gratitude expressed. Do not fail to use those final days and months, if you have the opportunity.

Some avoid it, and they regret it. Like the young husband told me thirty years ago, "I think we wasted so much time avoiding the chance to talk to each other, I wish I could have those last two months to live over.

With sudden death, life is over and gone before words can be spoken. It is especially troublesome if there has been some strain in the relationship. One of the longest roads to climb is back from a sudden death where all was not well when the death occurred. There, added to the grief, is the agony of the remembered argument and words that can never be recalled. I often advise my family, friends and parishioners, "Every time you say good bye, treat the other person as if you might never see them again. That way you will never have to live with a bad, bad memory."

A sudden death can be even more devastating when the loved one is far away when death occurs. Death at a distance is different, and in some ways more difficult to overcome. Being present can be helpful in the chance to absorb and come to grips with the passing. Seeing the body, as many experts say, usually helps us to bring some closure on the finality of death.

If the greatest mystery in life is death, then the greatest mystery of death is a sudden passing. Henry David Thoreau has a touching story in his little volume called <u>Recollections of Cape Cod</u>. He tells of a day, a Sunday morning in October 1849, when the St. John Brig, out of Galway Bay, was one mile from shore, and ran aground at Grampus Rock. The ship went down. One hundred forty-five people, women and children too, who were trying to immigrate to the New World, lost their lives in an instant. "They emigrated to a far newer world", Thoreau added, "than Columbus ever dreamed of, but one for which there is more evidence."

Then Thoreau, as only Thoreau could do, wrote: "I began to search for what it meant. As I watched the funeral directors coming, it occurred to me that those human beings were now mere bodies. What just a couple of moments ago had been the most precious thing on all the earth, one mile from shore, turned into nothing." Everyone who has experienced a sudden death of a loved one knows exactly what he means.

* * * *

The saddest case of sudden death in the Bible is the death of the prophet Ezekiel's wife. He was a faithful follower of God. He was loyal, good and true, as a prophet and a husband. He loved his wife. One Sabbath morning he preached his usual sermon, no doubt a good one; but then, he writes: "I spoke to the people in the morning, and that evening my wife died." (Ezekiel 24:18) He was devastated. Who knows what he might have done on his own, moped and mourned a while. But God commanded him to get on with his prophecy, and he did. Getting back to work, getting on with life is a good plan to follow. It was not easy. . .but he did it. Ezekiel went on to greater glory, prompted in large measure by the inspiration and memory of his wife. He lived to make her proud.

In more recent times, the great Scots preacher, Arthur Gossip, also preached the very Sunday after his wife had died. He ended his sermon with:

> *"And now back to life again, like a healthy-minded laddie at some boarding school, who, after the first day's hour of homesickness, resolves, if he is wise, he will not mope, but throw himself into the life about him, and do his part and play the game and enjoy every minute – aye, he does it, too – though always, always his eyes look ahead for the term's end, and always, always his heart thrills and quickens at the thought of that wonderful day when he will have not memories and letters only, but the whole of his dear ones really there, when he will be with them again and they with him. Well, that will come in time."*

(Gossip, <u>The Hero in Thy Soul</u>, p 115.)

● ● ● ●

In the Book of Acts, Chapter Five, there is another kind of sudden death. Ananias and his wife Sapphira had sold some property. Luke tells of the agreement which every Christian had made: To bring to the Apostles all of their profits, so the money could be distributed equally among the needy. This couple held part of the proceeds back. Simon Peter chastised them. Then, both in turn were so overcome with shock and remorse that they fell down in an instant and died, a shock to the heart as well as the soul.

The stress and pressures of life can exert enormous strain upon a person over short periods and long. The causes of sudden death are usually complicated. They have to do with genetic predispositions, and with how one cares for one's life and health. The body remembers what you do to it. Or, it can follow some traumatic event of the moment. Sudden death often follows times of tremendous exertion and anxiety.

So, how can a person best handle a sudden passing? There is another biblical passage, which offers a significant insight. It appears in Genesis 5. It comes at the time of Methuselah; the longest lived of all God's children. The author traces the earliest genealogy of created man: from Adam, through Seth and Enos, then to Jared, the father of Enoch.

Enoch was the father of Methuselah. He was a good and kindly, quite righteous man. Not much detail is given, but his life was so exceptional that he did not die a normal death. God took him immediately away to Himself. Genesis 5: 24 reads: "Enoch walked with God; and he was seen no more; for God took him." A lovely story, akin to the Ascension of Elijah, and of Jesus.

"He was seen no more." He went to "walk with God." That simple verse will give you great comfort and inner peace. Try to imagine that your loved one went out to walk with the Lord, as you might take a casual walk with your father or your favorite friend. "Why do you seek the living among the dead?" the Angel asked at the empty tomb on Easter, "He is not here, He is risen. . . ." He went for a walk with God!

One day we will all be together again. What is hidden, Jesus promised, will one day be made known. The Wisdom of Solomon says, "He who pleased God was loved. . . Having become completed in a short while. . .his soul was pleasing to the Lord. . .so God sped him away." (Chapter 9)

It was no doubt a massive shock for Enoch's wife and mother and children, but not for him. He was out taking a walk with God. One day they would join him, in God's good time. John Bunyan tells the story of Christian on his journey into heaven: "He passed over, and all

54

the trumpets sounded for him on the other side." Listen for the sound of the trumpets!

"The Pilgrims then began to inquire if there was no other way to the gate. And then they asked the men standing by if the waters were all of one depth. They replied.... 'No, you shall find it deeper or shallower, as you believe in the King of the place.'

"And entering the waters, Christian began to sink, and crying out to his friend Hopeful, he said, 'I sink in deep waters; the billows go over my head, all his waves go over me!'

"Then said the other, 'Be of good cheer, my brother, for I feel the bottom, and it is good.

"....I have formerly lived by hearsay, and faith, but now I go where I shall live by sight, and shall be with him in whose company I delight myself.'

"....So he passed over and all the trumpets sounded for him on the other side.

PILGRIM'S PROGRESS, JOHN BUNYAN

• • • •

The Scriptures warn us constantly of being ready, so that we will be prepared. Jesus said: "But of that day or that hour no one knows, not even the angels in heaven, nor the Son, but only the Father. Take heed, watch; for you do not know when the time will come. It is like a man going on a journey, when he leaves home, he puts his servants in charge, each with his work, and commands the doorkeeper to be on the watch. Watch therefore, for you do not know when the master of the house will come.

For Those Who Are Left Behind

"When St. Paul Said Goodbye. . ."
(II Timothy 4:6-8)

Here you have it, the first fine and wonderful Christian Saint summing up his life as the end came near: "The time of my departure has come." he wrote. A simple final statement: no regrets, no recriminations, no pleading for delays. My favorite author Annie Dillard wrote that "The dying never say 'please'; they always say 'thank you'." "There is a time for everything under the heavens," wrote the author of Ecclesiastes, "A time to be born and a time to die." That's it. When it comes, it's here. The real heroes of the Bible face death valiantly as a part of life, almost all of the time. As the poet wrote: "The coward dies a thousand deaths before his time; the valiant faces death but once."

Not one of us will live on earth forever. We do not choose the moment of our birth and we do not choose the moment of our death. There are often deep and abiding questions about when and why and how. But there is no question whatever that the hour of our departure will come.

Paul continued: "I have fought the good fight. I have finished the race. I have kept the faith." Proud and contented is the man or woman who can say that: "I did the best I could. It's over now. I'm tired and I want to go home. In looking back, I was not perfect, but I ran hard and stayed on course. So be it. I am ready to pass the baton along to someone else."

John Cowper Powyss wrote on life and death: "Let us imagine our old woman in her shawl and our old man with his walking stick, taking a brief stroll down the road.....Let us be bold enough to imagine our old friend advancing a little farther along the lane...We may suppose - for our friend is only too likely to be too infirm for long walks – that, as he turns to make for home, he catches sight of the historic river of that district, winding its way between the scattered homesteads...Old age has its own special advantage in such a case; it can let its mind dwell on the river *as* a river, dwell on the ancient mystery of that tide's winding flow...

..."They are taking advantage of their superannuation from work and play, from competition with their fellows, from responsibility *for* their fellows. Old age has set them free...Returning home past the familiar landmarks, they greet each gnarled and twisted tree-root that stretches into the ditch at their side as if it were a secret signal from old age to old age. As their fathers saw it they see it....Older than the meadows, older than the river, is this recurrent token of the coming on of night; and the very darkness itself that begins to descend upon them is felt in their present mood as it has been felt by others like them from the first twilights of time; felt as an infinite escape, as they shuffle home, from the wounding separations of all beginnings, into the healing absorbings of all ends." (The Art of Growing Older)

It's like a long walk on an autumn evening, when tired, but satisfied, near the end of the day they head for home, with a kindly thought of how sweet it will be to lie down to pleasant dreams.

* * * *

"So live, that when thy summons comes to join
The innumerable caravan, which moves
To that mysterious realm, where each shall take
His chamber in the silent halls of death.
Thou go not, like the quarry-slave at night,

Scourged to his dungeon, but, sustained and soothed
By an unfaltering trust, approach thy grave
Like one who wraps the drapery of his couch
About him, and lies down to pleasant dreams."

WILLIAM CULLEN BRYANT
"Thanatopsis"

Saint Paul adds: "Henceforth there is laid up for me the Crown of Righteousness which the Lord will award to me on that day. . ." Paul lived in the confidence that Christ would be there waiting, and Christ was. I am sure He will be now.

12

WHEN SUICIDE OCCURS

"From Abimelech to Judas. . ."

There are seven recorded suicides in the Bible, that we know of, only a couple of which are known among regular readers of the Scriptures. There are a variety of reasons why the suicides occurred.

First is Abimelech, an ancient Judge of Israel. He was a ruthless man. He had killed thousands of people, including some of his own brothers. Following a plot against his life, he was hit on the head by a millstone dropped by a woman from an upper window. He survived; but he was so ashamed of being wounded by a woman, he killed himself with his own sword. Shame brought an end to his life. In suicide, it often does. (Judges 9) I have seen it myself many times.

Second was Samson, also a Judge. Handsome and powerful, but he had a weakness for the women. Beautiful Delilah found the source of his strength. It was in his hair. She shaved his head. He lost his power. Blinded, he ended up in a Philistine prison. Later, at a huge celebration in their temple, he pushed the pillars down and killed himself along with everyone there. (Judges 13 ff.) Sometimes one sacrifices his life in behalf of what is good: A hero's death, provided you were not a Philistine.

Third, King Saul, a fine and mighty warrior and reigning monarch for years. But in the end, he lost his mind. He found his best self deserting him. In a moment of agony he fell on his own sword. He had every thing a man could want; but he couldn't handle himself and the terror inside. Often suicide is brought on by depression and mental illness, and the loss of self esteem. (I Samuel 31) In fact some say it always is.

Fourth, immediately following the King's death, Saul's Armor-Bearer killed himself. Terrified that his master was gone, and being afraid of what might happen to him next, he took his own life. Many people who commit suicide do so out of fear, all kinds of fear.

Fifth was Ahitophel, a counselor of great renown at the time of David. But, one day, after people refused to seek his advice any longer, it says, "Ahitophel went home and set his house in order." People intent on suicide often do. They take care of infinite details. Having lost respect, feeling rejected, Ahitophel killed himself. Rejection, real or imagined, is often the impetus for suicide. Be on the look out for those who "set their lives in order". (II Samuel 15)

Sixth was Zimri. Having lost his kingdom, he set fire to his palace and destroyed himself because of his sins. The feeling of guilt and shame is often too much to bear. If one feels he cannot bear to stand before God or to face others, it seems like the easiest way to end it all is to take one's own life. (I Kings 16)

The last recorded suicide in the Bible was Judas Iscariot. It is a familiar story. Judas had betrayed his Lord, for thirty shekels of silver. As it turned out, he was so distraught he tried to give the money back. The authorities refused to take it. He was disconsolate. He threw the coins away and he took his own life. Remorse is often in the background of suicide attempts. (Matthew 27 and Acts I. . .Do not be bothered by the fact that the stories do not agree as to how Judas did it. The fact is that he did.)

The suicide death of one you love brings a special sadness. Normally, those remaining feel guilty. "There was so many things I could have done to help him," she said, "but I got tired of all his crises. If I had only known this one was real." Many know that feeling. Guilt is common. So is anger; but neither is the final measure of a suicidal death. The one who takes his life, or hers, is ultimately responsible. It often is framed by mystery. But Christ understands, even when we do not. God can forgive a self-inflicted death. The church used to classify it as a "mortal sin", unforgivable, to be punished by the eternal fires of hell. Not so. One day, the Bible promises, we will all understand. "What is hidden will one day be made known."

So, go gently with yourself and your regrets. If someone you love takes his or her own life, do not blame yourself. The Church, and its theology, has often missed the point. The suicide victim is not condemned to hell. I wrote "victim" there on purpose. Often those who take their lives are victims of the stress and emotional pressures of their time. It can follow a long battle with mental illness. Almost everyone I know has taken a serious peek at the option. But have no fear; God in Christ can forgive them, and us. No one alive knows for sure, but Judas Iscariot could be in heaven. That is not our decision. We all betray the Lord. We all need His loving care. Surely the Bible teaches that Christ can and will forgive, if we repent, confess our sin and turn to Him.

13

THE DEATH OF A MOTHER. . .

"Sarah, The Mother of Isaac"

The name Sarah in Hebrew means "Noble Lady". This noble woman married Abraham not long after his father had died (Genesis 11). The marriage was not easy for Sarah. "She was barren", the Bible says bluntly, in a day when children, especially a male heir, were essential for the marriage to continue and the future to come.

It took a long, long time. So long that when she was finally told that she would have a child, she was so old, it says, "Sarah laughed out loud". But, in spite of the laughter, for which she was chastised, she bore a son. They named the boy Isaac. (Genesis 21) Life went on. Isaac grew. But since Sarah was of advanced years when her son was born, they were not destined to have long decades together. Isaac was still a young man when his mother was taken from him.

"Sarah died at Hebron, in the land of Canaan, after a good long life".... "Abraham went in to mourn and weep for her." (Genesis 23) The Hittites owned the land at that time. Abraham bought a family burial ground from them. He made it over to be suitable and he buried his wife in a cave among the trees of the field of Machpelah, a little east of Hebron. He and the other patriarchs are also buried there, in the Land of Shechem.

In his own advancing years, Abraham was concerned that their son

Isaac should be married to a good woman of the right faith. His servants went out at his command. With the help of the Lord, they found a beautiful young woman named Rebekah. She agreed, and they brought her back to Abraham's house. They met Isaac on the way. He fell in love at first sight. He and Rebekah were soon married, and, it says, "He loved her." That's nice. It adds, at the end of Chapter 23: Rebekah comforted Isaac "after his mother's death." Not much more to say. If you have never had the experience, you might pass the sentence by.

The death of a mother is an event of major importance in a life; especially for a son. It does not matter how old you are. Every parent-child exchange over the years has a variety of feelings attached to it. Sarah had not been a perfect mother. She had a bit of a jealous streak. She was at times overly protective of her son. She experienced some troubling times in her plans and worries about Isaac. But she loved him; and he loved her. When she was taken away he was lost.

His father married another woman after his wife died, almost instantly it appears. Father Abraham became immersed in a new time of joy and expectation, I guess. Seven additional sons were born to that new marriage. Isaac was left to make it on his own. . . Thank God Rebekah was there, with her loveliness, with her beauty and compassion. She was able to understand and comfort her young husband. Somehow she knew how to do it.

But, it is often difficult for a wife, or anyone else for that matter, to comfort a man whose mother has died. For one thing, men often choose not to share their inner thoughts and pain. They feel they must be "real men". They must not show their tears; that would be interpreted as weakness. To break through the mental and emotional barriers at so sensitive a time as a mother's death can be nearly impossible. If a man has not shared his weaknesses and tears along the way, he probably will not do it at this time. So his wife and children and friends must guess what is going on inside his head and heart.

Rebekah apparently was able to comfort Isaac by her patience and love. Isaac opened himself up to allow her to come into his soul and psyche. All husbands (all men) should try to do the same. There is no merit in being proud and strong, not when you hurt inside. There is no shame in tears. Jesus often wept, especially when his friend Lazarus died.

Mothers are special and unique. We each get only one. Others can, and often do, enter our lives with motherly graces. The Bible does not say enough about mothers. Maybe it is because all sixty-six Books were written by men. There is one majestic chapter, however, at the end of the Book of Proverbs. I leave it to you whose wives and mothers are gone:

> *"A good wife (woman) who can find?*
> *She is far more precious than jewels.*
> *The heart of her husband trusts in her,*
> *and he will have no lack of gain.*
> *She does him good, and not harm,*
> *All the days of her life.*
> *. . .She provides food for her household,*
> *. . .She opens her hand to the poor,*
> *and reaches out her hands to the needy.*
> *. . .Strength and dignity are her clothing,*
> *and she laughs at the time to come.*
> *She opens her mouth with wisdom,*
> *and the teaching of kindness is on her tongue.*
> *She looks well to the ways of her household,*
> *And does not eat the bread of idleness.*
> *Her children rise up and call her blessed;*
> *Her husband also, and he praises her:*
> *'Many women have done excellently,*
> *but you surpass them all.'*
> *Charm is deceitful, and beauty is vain,*
> *But a woman who fears the Lord*
> *Is to be praised.*
> *Give her of the fruit of her hands,*
> *And let her works praise her in the gates."*
> PROVERBS 31

14

THE DEATH OF A FATHER. . .

"When Elisha Lost His Friend and Father. . ."
(II Kings 2:1-15)

Hidden away in Second Kings is the story of the day the Lord took Elijah up to heaven. Elijah was the first of the great prophets. Elisha was his student. He always called Elijah "Father". Elijah probably was not his biological father. We do not know for sure. For our purposes, a series of important things happened on that day when Elisha lost the one he loved.

First, Elisha (the son) was faithful to the end. Elijah told him to leave, but he refused: "As the Lord lives, and you yourself live, I will not leave you." In the time nearing death, it helps to have a faithful friend or family member near-by. As many others know, there was joy for Elisha in being there to offer love and help, so his father would have someone to talk to, and that he would not be alone. You are lucky if you can be near your loved one in the final days and hours. So is the loved one. Too many of us, unlike the olden days, are far, far away. There is often one family member who lives near and bears the weight of all the immediate needs. That does not seem fair. Thank God for that son or daughter or friend who is "chosen" for special duty.

If you have waited and watched through a long lingering, never-ending illness, you know how he felt. Elisha did not want to lose his father. But the time had come. Elisha remained faithful. In looking back that is sometimes the most helpful feeling we can have: "I have no regrets. I was there. I remained faithful to the end."

Next Elijah said, "Ask what I shall do for you, before I am taken from you." What a powerful request from one about to leave this earth. We should all ask it. Elisha answered, "I pray you, let me inherit a double portion of your spirit." That is: Let me be like you. I want to carry on what you leave behind. I do not need the things you have. I do not want your money. I ask for the power and the peace to become your successor in the fine things of life, to carry on the treasures of our family and our faith in spiritual and moral matters, so that I will live to make you proud.

Most of us feel that way when our parents die, or when a favorite old friend is taken away. It is time for the next generation to take over. We need to carry on. Gone from our sight, but not gone from us. We want to live to carry on their memory.

• • • •

Next it says, Elijah was "taken up by a whirlwind into heaven". His son saw it and cried. It is all right to cry. Tears are the price you pay for love. If you had not become involved in the passage of another's life, it would be of no great concern at all. Tennyson caught it best of all in his poem.

"IN MEMORIAM"

Strong Son of God, immortal love
Whom we, that have not seen thy face,
By faith, and faith alone, embrace
Believing where we cannot prove.

Our little systems have their day,
They have their day and cease to be;
They are but broken lights of thee,
And Thou, O Lord, art more than they.

We have but faith: we cannot know;
For knowledge is of things we see;
And yet we trust it comes from thee,
A beam in darkness, let it grow.

Oh yet we trust that somehow good
Will be the final goal of ill.
That nothing walks with aimless feet;
That not one life shall be destroyed,
When God hath made it all complete.

That loss is common would not make
My own less bitter, rather more;
Too common! Never morning wore
To evening, but that some heart did break.

I hold it true, what'er befall;
I feel it, when I sorrow most;
'Tis better to have loved and lost
Than never to have loved at all.

(TENNYSON)

• • • •

I encourage people to allow grief to have its way. Jesus wept when his friend Lazarus died. What was good enough for the Savior is good enough for you and me. There is no merit in pretending to manage death well, on the outside. Delayed grief, as we have said, can be the source of much greater agony later on. Elisha knew how to do it. He cried. He rent his clothes in pieces, an Old Testament sign of mourning. Well done, Elisha!

• • • •

But watch what happens next: It says: Elisha took up the mantle, the cape of prophecy, which had fallen from Elijah. He put it over his shoulders, and he went back to the banks of the Jordan. That means no he did not grieve forever, even if he never forgot his father. He kept going. He asked for the Spirit of Elijah and received it.

Then, he struck the waters with the mantle of Elijah. The waters parted, a miracle, just like the miracles of Elijah. I think applause was heard in heaven, or at least a great Amen! It is hard to say goodbye to someone that you love, but if you can determine to do your part to carry on, to finish their unfinished business, it can all work out in time.

Finally it says, "When the sons of the prophets saw him, they said, 'The Spirit of Elijah rests upon Elisha.'" I love the story and its ending. It tells us what to do, and how to do it, when we lose someone we love. So live that others will see the spirit of the one you love resting on you. Pray that it will last forever.

> "...*Take up our quarrel with the foe:*
> *To you from falling hands we throw*
> *The torch; be yours to hold it high.*
> *If you break the faith with us who die*
> *We shall not sleep, though poppies grow*
> *In Flanders fields.*"
> "IN FLANDERS FIELDS"
> JOHN MCCRAE

PART III

"LIFE IS LIKE A TALE THAT IS TOLD. . ."

Psalm 90 has a lovely verse: "Life is like a tale that is told", just like a story. Think of the stories you have heard, or read. Some are long. Some are short and end too soon. I envy those who have not yet read my favorite stories. Some are beautiful and lovely. Others are sad and filled with puzzlement. Some stories end happily; we call them comedies. Others end sadly; we call them tragedies. Some stand out like a beautiful flower at the head of a garden. Others flourish fast and disappear. Life is like a tale that is told.

The Psalmist knew that the main thing about a story is that the author has the right to tell it. If the story lingers on long after the point is made, or if it leaves us bothered with its too soon ending, still, it is the author's tale to tell. Hemmingway did not write like Thomas Wolfe: he was brief and to the point. Wolfe decorated his novels with words and purple prose. I like both of them..

It is the same with our lives. God is the author. He gives us freedom, but he sets the boundaries. He allows us to develop and grow and tell our stories, but ultimately the script belongs to Him. He is in charge. The story moves along, and one day ends. We have our individual parts to play, but God writes the story.

Sometimes we wish that life were different. How we wish that we could take the happiest of our moments and save them for all our days. Would that we could avoid the passing of those we love too much to lose. But we know our lives too well to lift that prayer. We must live the life we have been given, not the one we long for. The story one day ends. But it does not really. It goes on and on. The ultimate in wonder is the Life in Christ that never ever ends.

So when your time comes, when you are forced to say goodbye, or when you lose someone you love, ponder the tale that was told. Think of all the good times. Focus on what death can never take away. Then accept the life you have to live; and go on to others who need you and love you still. Pray for Christ to take you by the hand and lead you on. For now and evermore. Amen.

PART IV

"A PEEK AT THE LAST PAGE"...

People often ask me "What happens when we die?" Sometimes they want to know whether we go straight to heaven; or, do we wait in the ground, as St. Paul writes in I Thessalonians 4, until Jesus returns. Sometimes the widow asks "Do you think Charlie will be there waiting for me when I die?" Many mourners have wanted to know if those who are gone know what is going on, on earth. "Can they see us?", or ultimately, "Can they communicate with those left behind?" If I say "yes", they want to know why those who are gone do not choose to exercise or initiate that heavenly communication more often than they do.

At times the focus of the question changes and becomes more theoretical, like "Do you believe in purgatory, Reverend? Doesn't it make sense that there should be a place where in-between people go"... like those who were a bit devilish, and disrespectful of some of the moral and spiritual rules; but not so bad, or irreversibly evil that they deserve eternal damnation? In Catholic theology Purgatory is for those who have committed venial sins, as opposed to mortal sins. Purgatory is an important doctrine, especially in the Roman Catholic tradition. It is worth some deep thought and study, even if it is not so critical for us here.

In the case of little children who die at birth, or as infants, there seems to be a need to have somewhere for them to go. In traditional Christian theology that place is called limbo, for children, Limbo/Infantum. It is an intermediate or transitional place where infants are not left alone. I prefer to believe that God in his mercy accepts infants and children directly to himself, in heaven. I see no need for them to be assigned to a limbo because they have not been baptized, but it is a time-honored tradition.

• • • •

Well, we have strayed form our point. We were discussing the variety of ways in which people have asked me through the years about what happens when we die. One of the most difficult ones for me to answer was a family time, a long while ago. My mother asked me a question one afternoon in 1985, 33,000 feet up in the sky, flying together on USAir from Pittsburgh to Florida, after my brother and father had passed away. It was her first flight in all her life. As she clutched her little nitroglycerine bottle in one hand, and my left hand in the other, she looked out the window and innocently asked me, "Well, where is it Richard?" I said, "Where is what?" She said "Heaven, isn't it supposed to be up here somewhere?" She, as many, if not the most of us, had grown up believing that heaven was supposed to be up, hell was down, and the earth was in between, an orderly three-tiered universe. Now I want you to know my mother was not naïve about life and death, she was bright and well read. But the temptation to quiz her ministerial son was too great to pass up, as she thought up things to make the flight go faster.

I said I didn't know, not for sure anyway. I told her heaven was a concept, a place where we would be with the Lord, our idea of the quintessential land of paradise. But I said I learned in seminary that it was not a spatial concept, not a floating empire on a raft of clouds. I volunteered that it was not necessarily 'up' and Hades 'down'. "Then, where is it?" she asked. To satisfy her I ended the discussion by saying it was likely farther up, farther than an airplane could go. That seemed to end the conversation, even if I caught in the corner of her eyes and voice, the sort of reservation, and rebuke a son or daughter often notices; in this case it asked something like, "Do you mean your father and I sent you to college, Theological Seminary and four more years of graduate school for your Ph.D., and you still don't know where heaven is?" I smile when I think about her question to this day.

• • • •

Let me take you to the Bible again and try to work out an answer to the question. Actually it is not as easy as it sounds, even for the most gifted theologian. The problem is that there is a line of development in the Doctrine of Eschatology (The Last Things) which stretches out the subject. I will over-simplify it for us here, but I take the following to be accurate and true to the Bible.

It might surprise you that there is not a unanimous and definitive word in all the Scriptures about what happens when we die. There are several different ideas, many with apparently equal credence. At times the Bible says that the dead will fall asleep until judgment day arrives, the final day. Then the graves will be opened, and we will each appear before the judgment seat of God. At other times the Bible says that we will remain in the ground unto Jesus Christ returns at the Second Coming. At still other times, it seems that we will go directly to heaven.

• • • •

There is no way to pull all these ideas together into a single belief. We must rest content with what we have been taught. Being a Presbyterian Pastor, I am mindful of what John Calvin wrote in his study of "The Last Things": "Now it is neither lawful nor expedient to inquire too curiously concerning our souls intermediate state....It is foolish and rash to inquire concerning unknown matters more deeply than Christ permits us to know. Scripture goes no father than to say that Christ is present with the deceased. They will receive blessed rest...but all things will be held in suspense until Christ the Redeemer appears." Amen.

• • • •

In the early years and centuries of the Old Testament the concept of living on forever is not a primary concern. There appears to be a universal idea that death does not mean the end of life. "Sheol" is a place which is neither heaven nor hell; neither is it a purgatory where the sins of earth are being worked on or worked out by prayers or punishment.

In the early Scriptures, those who have died seem to be in Sheol. For example, when Jacob was distraught because he believed his son Joseph was dead; he said, "I shall go down to Sheol, to my son, mourning.: (Genesis 37:35). Following Korah's rebellion in the book of Numbers, it says, as Moses had predicted, "...They and all that belonged to them went down alive to Sheol; and the earth closed over them...(Numbers 16:33)

The best-known example of all is the time when Saul went to a medium and asked her to "divine" up the spirit of Samuel who was deceased. She did. When the vision came, "Saul knew that it was Samuel, and he bowed his face to the ground and did obeisance." (I Samuel 28:14)

We could go on and on. Sheol is mentioned sixty-four times in the Old Testament. It appears to be a place where souls gather under the watchful eye of God. It is underground. It is not a literal Hell but neither is it a heavenly place as in the New Testament. It is mainly a place for the dead to go and remain.

• • • •

However, there is another essential belief in the early Hebrew Scriptures. It was essential to remember those who were gone. Remember, in the Old Testament, immortality was not an important concern. The continuation of God's people and their faith was paramount. The Chosen People must continue to be faithful as a community. When Abraham passed away, it says he was gathered to his fathers, as his son would later be gathered to him. When Jacob died it reads simply, "He breathed his last." His primary concern was not to go to heaven, but to make sure that each of his twelve sons and the tribes of Israel for which they were named, would not forget him or his fathers or their faith. So long as someone remembered you and carried on your name and faith, you were not gone from the earth. By their remembrance, you became part of the continuing company of God's people.

• • • •

Later, in the Old Testament, things began to change, partly because of what happened when God's people went into exile. By then, with Jerusalem destroyed and the survivors of God's people away in Babylon, they could no longer be gathered to their fathers; that is, it was too far to the land where their fathers were buried.

So there arises a concept of personal immortality. Out of his fallen life on earth, e.g., Job said that "without his flesh he would see God." Daniel wrote that those "who sleep in the desert" will awake. Best known of all is in the thirty-seventh Chapter of Ezekiel, where the dry bones came to life. The dead were not dead. Ezekiel peeked over the top of the highest mountain in the world and came back to tell us that they live on forever more. The bones are connected and there is life and joy in the Valley of the Dead. And King David said on the death of his son, "He shall not come back to me; I shall go to him."

• • • •

When we come to the New Testament, I wish I could tell you it becomes absolutely clear. Unfortunately, it does not. Curiously, there is very little teaching from Jesus about the afterlife. In the synoptic Gospels, Matthew, Mark, and Luke, His references to eternity are part of a larger teaching. We have mentioned Matthew 25 where the sheep will be separated from the goats. His previous mention that there would be no marriages in heaven comes in answer to the question about the woman who had seven husbands and whose wife would she be beyond the grave. He said there were no marriages in heaven. There can be no doubt that Jesus believed in the everlasting life, which was also common in the tradition of the Pharisees. He believed that God's people will be rewarded by what they do. He stated that He was "The Way, The Truth and The Life". But in the Synoptic Gospels He seems to have been far more concerned about what we do on earth to bring the Kingdom of God. The Kingdom continues on in the afterlife, but it begins in the here and now.

• • • •

It was not until St. Paul began to write his letters about twenty-five years after Jesus' death, that the issue took on a new character. I am not reissuing the old argument which said that Paul differed with Jesus. To me, it is only a further development. Paul had to reassure the believers that Jesus would not forget the ones who had already died. In I Corinthians 15 he raises the discussion to a different level when he explores the highest reaches of the Resurrection, where we shall all be changed. "What is sown is physical, he writes, "what is raised is spiritual." He does not tell us what that means exactly, but anyone can assume that a physical body does not survive its own death. Jesus survived his as the Son of God, but that is what Easter is all about. The angel said to the women, "Why do you seek the living among the dead? He is not here. He is risen, as He said."

• • • •

My personal belief, culled out from all I have written here is that Judgment Day will come for each and all of God's children. Otherwise what we do here and now does not seem to matter quite so much. But, I have a personal idea about what will happen on Judgment Day. I feel certain it is compatible with what is taught in the Bible.

When the final Judgment Day comes….Whatever else might be unclear to you or me or anyone at all about what happens to us after we have breathed our last, the Bible, Old Testament and New, from Genesis to Revelation, is quite explicit and insistent that we will each and all appear before the judgment seat of Almighty God, to give an accounting of what we did and did not do throughout our years on earth. "And just once it is appointed for men to die once, and after that comes judgment" (Hebrews 9:27) Romans 14:10 adds "For we shall all stand before the judgment seat of God; …each of us shall give account of himself to God."

So, if you worry about that day; if the memories of things you never should have said or done keep cropping up; if you fear what God, the Righteous Judge, might say or do to you; if you keep trying to figure out how God will work it out for your loved one now gone; then pause with me before we close out this little book on losing one you love, and let me take it up a station higher. We did not go far enough in our quotation from Hebrews 9:27. Verse 28 continues "So Christ having been offered once to bear the sins of many, will appear a second time, not to deal with sin but to save those who are eagerly waiting for him."

Matthew 25 tells the story of judgment in a familiar tale. It reads: "When the son of man comes in his glory, and all the angels with him, then he will sit on his glorious throne. Before him will be gathered all the nations, and he will separate them one from another as a shepherd separates the sheep from the goats."

The righteous who inherited the Kingdom will be admitted by Christ on the basis of what they each had done to feed the poor, to visit the sick, to care for those who needed help. He said "If you have done it unto one of the least of these my brethren, you have done it unto me."

To those on his left hand he will say "Depart from me, for you did not care for me when I needed you." They asked "Lord when did we see you hungry or thirsty or a stranger or naked or sick or in prison, and did not minister to you?" He answered them, "If you did not do it to one of the least of these, you did not do it to me." And, they were sent away.

• • • •

Many people oversimplify the way in which in the Bible says we are admitted to Eternal life. They insist that we say this word or that word, always their words, lifted from selected passages in the New Testament. They condemn all who do not repeat their chosen jargon.

The Bible is not so narrow or so final as some pretend it is. I think it is a matter of believing that Jesus the Christ is God Incarnate, the Son of God, to whom the Lord has entrusted the keys to the kingdom. The Bible is clear that salvation comes only through Christ. It does.

But, that does not mean that our Lord is limited to what mortal beings say must be said or done by the people of the earth in order to win His approval and gain entrance to eternity. When Peter was preaching in Acts 10, he noted that God "commanded us to preach to the people, and to testify that he is the one ordained by God to be the Judge of the living and the dead." There will be a Judgment Day.

But, I repeat, it is Jesus Christ who has the right to determine who will receive the gift of Eternal Life and on what terms. It is on his terms. For example, on the cross, Jesus said to one of the criminals hanging beside him, "Truly, I say to you, today you will be with me in Paradise." (Luke 23:43). The convicted thief had just rebuked the other criminal being crucified, "We are guilty", he said, "but this man was innocent." (23:41) There was no confession of faith, no giving of his life to Jesus, just an observation that the King of the Jews had done no wrong at all.

James asks bluntly, "What does it profit...if a man says he has faith but not works? Can his faith save him? If a brother or sister is ill-clad and in lack of daily food, and one of you says to them, 'Go in peace, be warmed and filled', without giving them the things needed for the body, what does it profit? So faith by itself, if it has no works, is dead." (James 2: 14-17) He is saying, as Jesus seems to have said in Matthew twenty-five, that you cannot find salvation just by reciting some words about what you say you believe. It is also a matter of what you have done.

In Matthew seven we read "Not every one who says to me, 'Lord, Lord', shall enter the Kingdom of heaven, but he who does the will of my father who is in heaven. On that day many will say to me, 'Lord, Lord, did we not prophesy in your name, and cast out demons in your name, and do many mighty works in your name?' And then I will declare to them, 'I never knew you; depart from me, you evil doers.'" (Matthew 7:2-23)

• • • •

There could be many surprises when that great and final Judgment Day shall come. Some who talked the best game of belief might hear the words of rebuke, others, who were not part of the confessional crowd, might hear kind and reassuring words. The keys to the kingdom have been given to Jesus Christ the Son. But he can open the gates of ever-lasting life to anyone and everyone he chooses.

• • • •

Fred Speakman, an old friend of mine now gone, said that he liked to think of Judgment Day as a courtroom trial in heaven. You (or I) will be the defendant in the trial. All those who wish to testify against the defendant will be the witnesses for the prosecution. God himself will be the Judge, seated high on The Throne. The prosecuting attorney has the long list of faults and foibles, failures and sins for us all. Oh dear, it will be a long day at trial, listening and waiting and wondering as the misdeeds of the days and decades of our lives are paraded before the court: much embarrassment and shock, some regret and remorse, no doubt a touch of fear....No one seems to be there to speak for the defense. "Will anyone appear as a witness for me? I tried hard. I did my best. I wish someone would stand up....Who will speak for the defense?"

Then, just at the moment of my deepest consternation, feeling alone and blue and depressed that the process does not seem fair, a person will arise from the back of the courtroom, and in a calm, deep, reassuring voice, say: "The defendant is a friend of mine. I can vouch for him. I will plead his case. I promise to take care of him forevermore."

The voice you will hear belongs to Jesus Christ. He knows our mortal frame; He became one of us; He was tempted in all ways such as we. He knows what it is to be a human being, frail and fragile as we are. And, while He never failed, He understands why we do.

It still might not seem fair, but the weight of evidence has shifted. It might seem partial, but it turns out that the defense attorney is the Son of the Judge. They sit beside each other in the heavenly realm. They are on the best of terms. You belong to Christ; He belongs to the Father. Everything is going to work out right.

Finally, the Judge says, "Thank you my Son. Open up the gates for the ones you choose, for now and evermore!" Amen.

PART V

POEM FOR THE LIVING

When I am dead,
Cry for me a little.
Think of me sometimes,
But not too much.
It is not good for you
Or your wife or your
Husband or your children
To allow your thoughts to dwell
Too long on the dead.
Think of me now and again
As I was in life,
At some moment which
It is pleasant to recall.
But, not for long.
Leave me in peace,
And I shall leave
You, too, in peace.
While you live,
Let your thoughts
Be with the living.

ANCIENT INDIAN PRAYER

PART VI

Selected Bible Readings

Genesis 1:1-31 . . . . The world God made is good
Genesis 49:28-50:10 . . . . The death of Jacob
Joshua 1:1-10 . . . . God will be with you
II Samuel 1:11-27 . . . . The death of Jonathan
I Kings 2:1-4 . . . . A father's final words
II Kings 2:1-4 . . . . The death of Elijah
Job 38 ff. . . . . God's answer to Job's "Why"
Psalm 8 . . . . The glory of man
Psalm 23 . . . . The Shepherd's Psalm
Psalm 24 . . . . The earth is the Lord's
Psalm 39:4-13 . . . . This fleeting life
Psalm 46 . . . . God is our refuge and strength
Psalm 90 . . . . As the generations pass
Psalm 103 . . . . Blessings of the Lord
Psalm 121 . . . . Lift up your eyes
Proverbs 31:10-31 . . . . A good woman
Ecclesiastes 3:1-15 . . . . A time to die
Isaiah 40:1-11 . . . . Comfort, comfort my people
Isaiah 43:1-7 . . . . Fear not
Ezekiel 37:1-10 . . . . The dry bones come to life
Matthew 5:1-14 . . . . The Beatitudes
Matthew 28:1-10 . . . . The Easter Story
John 14:1-12 . . . . Let not your hearts be troubled
Romans 8:28-39 . . . . What shall we say to these things
I Corinthians 13 . . . . The gift of love

READINGS FROM THE APOCRYPHA